I0436949

For Freedom and Democracy

(The Unloved Letters of a Likeable Libertarian)

Dr. Steven Parris Ward

Copyright © 2013 by Dr. Steven Parris Ward.

Library of Congress Control Number:		2013900925
ISBN:	Hardcover	978-1-4797-8058-7
	Softcover	978-1-4797-8057-0
	Ebook	978-1-4797-8059-4

All rights reserved. No part of this book may be reproduced or transmitted in any form or by any means, electronic or mechanical, including photocopying, recording, or by any information storage and retrieval system, without permission in writing from the copyright owner.

This book was printed in the United States of America.

To order additional copies of this book, contact:
Xlibris Corporation
0-800-644-6988
www.xlibrispublishing.co.uk
Orders@xlibrispublishing.co.uk
305798

For Freedom and Democracy (The Unloved Letters of a Likeable Libertarian) is a series of letters that were moderated, reviewed, censored or automatically published on the Daily Telegraph blog site in response to various articles written by the esteemed journalists therein. Commenting on the various topics of the changing political situation, its twists, turns and deceits, they focus chiefly on the rise of UKIP, the decline of David Cameron PM (Pre-Mortem), his Europhile buccaneers, and last but not least, the emergence of the dominating, corrupt and undemocratic European Union.

These witty, serious, succinct, detailed and on occasion humorous letters, chart the duplicities of both the Press, and the people they claim to criticise and report, with a blunt and curt analysis of the current contemporary political situation. The letters reflect the decline of national state democracy, the emergence of politically correct bigotry, and the rise of the European autocratic mega state.

This book is dedicated to Peter Hitchens; one of the few journalists of sanity in an ever increasing world of useful idiots, Liberal lefties and conspiratorial mad men.

He is a lone voice: a John the Baptist, a solitary prophet crying in the cultural wilderness. A Christian ascetic amidst the Socialist scorpions and Marxist maelstroms. A British colonial- a modern day Augustine- who whilst witnessing the sack of Rome from afar gives nostalgic commentary on Britain's decline, with his visionary eye still fixed on the shining city on a heavenly hill.

"Now is the time to think seriously about our future in Europe – to discuss where Britain fits in, and what role we should play. That should be for the British people to decide in a referendum, something that may not happen any time soon." – response to David Davis, The Daily Telegraph (14 Dec 2011).

I think most sensible, freedom loving, democratically minded citizens have given this plenty of thought. It isn't acceptable for David Davis to simply suggest 'we just need to think about it, so that some time down the line (perhaps in three or four years) we can perhaps have a referendum'. Sorry Mr Davis, that is the standard party line we have been fed with from both Labour and Conservative apparatchiks for decades. It has been given by successive governments, and it just isn't good enough. It has caused many who seek freedom from the EU to become rightly disenchanted, and deeply so until the veto. The Prime Minister's stance, incorporated in the party's "now is not quite the right time" attitude, needs to change.

The extraordinary crisis and circumstances of late have revealed the EU for what it truly is: an emerging federal autocratic tyranny of totalitarian aspirations. This encapsulates an agenda moving towards dictatorial rule. Yes the EU consists of a parliament ruled by a Commission, but the Commission is in effect no more than an undemocratic cabal of unelected federalist bureaucrats. These Eurocrats instruct a democratic European Parliament about what to legislate and what to rubber-stamp. The Parliament, therefore, has little power to properly introduce or revoke legislation in that rather worrying set up. It is no more than a Supreme Soviet style Parliament taking orders from an EC Politburo. A Commission which, in effect, is a corrupt oligarchy. Add to this the ECB/ IMF intergovernmental pressure groups; who are aligned to it with vested financial interests and a globalist agenda, along with the cabal which is the Frankfurt Group, and the deception of democracy is complete.

Now, with recent developments, EU has shown its true colours and future agenda to be one of federal tyranny. A close knit, undemocratically appointed cabal, which seeks to rule sovereign nations from a centralised body, imposing automatic sanctions, whilst removing fiscal autonomy and even the right to vote. It justifies these measures due to an economic crisis it largely engineered itself. It has displayed with the Fiscal Compact and Lisbon Treaty no real concern for the democratic rights or sovereignty of nations at all. Nor has it displayed concern for the rights of the individual.

It has displayed intolerance to any that might oppose it; whether they be Prime Minister or common citizen. We have been faced with demands to accept, or face the consequences: sneering Presidents, jeering MEP's, racist slurs suggesting "Anglo-Saxon" plots; such cajoling to compliance has been endured, and all for creating a euro crisis it falsely claims we caused. Our citizens have even been demeaned and ridiculed as "Island Monkeys". Is this the reaction for requesting modest proposals which sought to merely slow down a repressive taxation strategy of a fiscal compact without true representation, and a fanatical integration agenda?

The citizens of this country deserve and demand a full in/out referendum. It is required as a sign that proves the integrity of our politicians, as well as our national status as a free democracy. Otherwise, the suspicions that our leaders are no more than mere cohorts working in cahoots with those unelected, federalist Commissars will become increasingly more prevalent.

As austerity measures bite, we can only hope suspicions do not turn to demonstrations of a more violent nature in this country, as they have already in other Southern member states such as Greece. It is up to the politicians to take this as their sacred responsibility; both to the people, and as a protection of our noble history as the "Mother of Modern Democracy". If they should err, they indeed may have to take responsibility for the terrible consequences that might ensue.

In a coded attack the Prime Minister warned that the Church must "keep on the agenda that speaks for the whole country" and that "moral neutrality was unacceptable". The Prime Minister's criticism of the Archbishop of Canterbury, Telegraph (17/12/2011).

The problem Mr Cameron is that Christianity doesn't speak for the whole country, or even the majority of the country anymore. It doesn't speak for the Sikhs and the Muslims, the Hindus and the Buddhists, the Jains and the Jews. It doesn't speak for the atheists or the agnostics. With its slanted leaning towards a politically correct agenda however, the Church of England now appears to have more in common with the ideologies of the radical agitators and Marxist ideologies that once professed it an opiate and a danger to the class consciousness of the people. It covertly seeks to implement the doctrines of Herbert Marcuse, rather than the theology of Saint Paul, or the teachings of Jesus the Nazarene.

Mr. Cameron has said "moral neutrality" is unacceptable. In this, I am in agreement. But the problem with that view is it supposes there is such a thing as a universal morality: a universal right and wrong, over and above the differing religious ideologies that express it. It supposes this can be communicated irrespective of the differing interpretations of what it is to practise. Accepting that there is a universal morality that informs moral relativism; how is it to be determined through the prism of faith? Should we love thy neighbour, or practise an eye for eye? Is it good to worship a sacred cow, or sacrifice it? Must we render unto Caesar what is Caesar's, or sympathise with our anarchist demonstrators on the steps of St Paul's?

In an attempt to speak to the masses, the Archbishop finds himself seeking to preach a universal, more populist message. A message that transcends one faith. In order, one suspects, to address dwindling congregation numbers, as well as maintain at least some semblance of multicultural harmony. The result, unfortunately, is moral neutrality. A neutrality that leads to ambiguity. When articulated, it becomes largely irrelevant and impotent; in order, one suspects, to protect and not offend other religious ideologies.

Perhaps it would be better for State and Religion to be separate (as inferred in the first amendment of the USA), but I personally would not want it to be at the expense of our historic traditions, or our monarchy's role as Defender of Faith. Perhaps, then, politics should attempt rather more to speak to the masses than religion, which is after all a question of personal faith.

The characteristic of the Church of England is one that sought to rid itself of the political imposition of rule by the Vatican and the Catholic Church. It should, therefore, not seek to impose or influence political legislation, nor should it seek to speak for the whole of the country. The Church, therefore, should confine itself to the role of addressing the moral needs of the individual who particularly professes a belief in Christianity. In this, politics should confine itself to an agenda which is areligious, and indeed seek to speak democratically for the majority of the country. Its concern for determining moral behaviour should not be for anything more than a concern with the proposal of judicial legislation, legal practise, and the compliance of British law. The Queen in her role as Defender adequately serves in her role as intermediary between the two.

The problem with both politicians and clergy is, whilst oft speaking in opposition, they too often consider they are universal moral arbiters, who have carte blanche to blame each other for moral and political failings. In this, their actions or belief systems are often found to be wanting or lacking in respect of themselves.

It is a pity moreover that the present Church of England is indicative of a more covert political ideology, which appears to have little or no true sympathy with many of the Biblical doctrines it previously espoused, through centuries of tradition and the principal tenets of the Bible. Its bizarre sympathies in some quarters to same sex marriage and homosexuality- an oft repeated prohibition and Biblical sin- being a case in point. Moreover, its recent sympathies with the Occupy movement against its own interests, displays a political bias that furthers the cause of the anti-capitalist stance. A stance that rather favours a Cultural Marxist agenda. This is readily proved, and should be read in conjunction with the next letter.

The Communist Roots of Occupy Wall Street.

A few weeks after its launch, Occupy Wall Street sought the financial services of the Alliance for Global Justice (AGJ) as its fiscal sponsor to manage online donations. AGJ was originally established to support the communist dictatorship in Nicaragua, and it continues to underwrite and promote the activities of Marxist movements in Central America. AGJ receives funding from a number of notable Left-wing foundations, including George Soros's Open Society Institute and Tides.

The U.S. financial crisis is not the cause of the Occupy Wall Street protests, for it is merely a tactic in the Long March to Communist revolution. The OWS movement does not seek financial reforms that would address the two principal causes of the collapse. It does not seek to reinstate the Glass-Stegall Act, nor does it recommend restricting bank loans to credit-worthy customers. What it does desire is a revolutionary overthrow of the capitalist system.

The OWS agenda was built on the groundwork that radical leaders had been laying for decades. One of them was Wade Rathke- a Sixties veteran. Rathke had worked with the National Welfare Rights Organization (NWRO), which aimed to "break" the welfare system by recruiting people to overwhelm its payment systems, and by inciting the invasion of its offices, often violently, to make additional demands for payments that could not be met.

In the early 1970s Rathke founded ACORN, soon to become the largest radical organisation in America. ACORN's specialty was voter fraud; conceived as a strategy to break the electoral system, ACORN activists also provided a powerful force behind Barack Obama's rise to the Senate in 2004, and his election to the White House in 2008.

Obama expressed sympathy for the movement, saying that he "understands the frustrations that are being expressed" by the protesters. Speaking in New Hampshire, he told Occupy supporters, "You are the reason I ran for office."

Nancy Pelosi lauded the movement as "young," and "spontaneous". Apparent spontaneity for Occupy was in fact orchestrated by a long-established network of Marxist and Communist 60's radical activists such as Kalle Lasn, Wade Rathke founder of ACORN, and Left Wing Communist radical Frances Fox Piven.

Piven had come up with the "break-the-system" strategy that Rathke's welfare strategy adopted. The strategy sought to overload the welfare system until it virtually bankrupted New York. Following New York's welfare fiasco, Piven escalated her scheme into a strategy to overload other government agencies with impossible demands, in order to create social chaos and economic collapse.

On the EU and the Euro crisis: 18th December 2011.

The insanity of ministers in all three parties is they actually believe it is in British interests to contribute to keeping this corrupt EU Leviathan alive. They label people who object to this growing federal EUSSR monster: "fruitcakes", or "swivel eyed loonies". In this, they engage in tit for tat bickering with member nations, before opening their purses ever wider to show they are truly sorry. They even now are planning ways to give more fiat money to the EU's ravenous appetite. They do this falsely, to keep it from dying the death it deserves. They pour more billions into its open mouth in the name of fiscal stability, whilst they continue to espouse political unity: a mere power grab to maneuver for greater, more undemocratic powers. They do this whilst they seek to pocket the benefits for themselves. It is a madness in any case, which appears to be promoting social and economic chaos in the name of the political ideology of collectivism.

We are witnessing the death of democratic accountability. Our ministers to their shame refuse citizen's demands for a referendum to leave, claiming they know what is in our best interests. They think only of themselves, their finances and their careers. The ultimate end for Britain must, and can only be, a simple trade agreement of an EFTA type, if national state democracy is to survive.

Yours

(for freedom and democracy)

Steven Parris Ward.

On the lobby group "Businesses for the New Europe" and its anti-democratic agenda: 19th December 2011.

"Businesses for the New Europe" is a politically biased lobby group. It seeks to promote the message of the EU by proxy for the benefit of a few select, big business men. It does this for the good of their future monopolies. They achieve this through the perpetuation of the corrupt and financially unaccountable EU, that cares nought for genuine freedom and democracy. It lobbies some impressive names. Yet this is a lobby group that champions the EU federal bloc. A bloc that stifles small businesses, and indeed destroys competitiveness between member state economies as it continues to develop its mega state.

This is not an organisation that champions the old European model of a single market (EEC), but one that promotes the "New Europe" of undemocratic federalism. A lobby group that promotes anti-democratic, appointed member Commissioners: Eurocrats who haven't been elected by the people. A lobby group that seeks to champion the European Commission; that oligarchic group that wields power in the name of integration and federalism. A lobby group that supports an unaccountable Europe, and one that is financially corrupt; for it hasn't been properly audited in 18 years.

This lobby group supports a Europe that has taken away habeas corpus and the presumption of innocence, favouring instead corpus juris, and one that is hell bent on destroying national sovereignty. A Europe which Herr Westerwelle said yesterday "is our common destiny to be part of". This appears to be irrespective of whether the majority of people in this country want it or not.

A lobby group that acts for such political aims does not act for the interests of Britain's democracy, freedom and sovereignty. Nor does it act for the good of the majority of its people. It does not act for the good of the country's Parliament, nor indeed the political parties that are housed in it. Indeed, it only acts as a support group for a European tyranny. Such a tyranny has the legal power, via the Lisbon Treaty, to be able to replace and dissolve political parties and leaders should they be deemed unsuitable, or should they pose a threat to its own best future interests. It has the power to destroy the affluence of the free market with its philosophy of wealth distribution that creates equality of outcome, but not equality of opportunity.

The "New Europe" stands for more than merely a single market of trade along EEC lines; for the latter is a model of the "old Europe", not the "new". In this they try to make out that kind of single market isn't possible without political and fiscal integration, when the truth is we have been part of that kind of European trade model for decades. They shouldn't make out the Euro is indispensable for that kind of trade model either, when it isn't. They shouldn't suggest that we must "do everything in our power to guarantee its viability" when shackling differing GDP's within the construct of a single currency is doomed to failure. The sane, long term course clearly requires a return to national currencies and a devaluation.

Do they then act to serve the interest of British citizens and promote British business interests, or do they promote only their own? The answer must be on the whole the latter. Mr Branson lives in the Caribbean and has just moved his Virgin brand company to Switzerland to avoid UK taxes. He has been a champion of off shore call centres in India for years at the expense of British jobs. Mr Sorrell moved his company to Dublin to avoid UK taxes. Mr. Brittan is a failed 1980s politician who became an EU Commissar. He may just be worried about his EU pension. Mr Rudd used to be a board member of the organisation "Britain in Europe". Its former title, which also falsely claimed political impartiality, was later linked to Labour's pro EU media campaign. It too was formed to get Britain into the Euro. So, one way or another, he too might well be on the EU payroll.

Finally, of course, no one wants to see economies suffer when the euro collapses. Thus, financially speaking, it is not in anyone's short term interests: it is not in the Euro-zone's, nor indeed in Britain's. In this respect Mr. Clegg, we Euro-sceptics are not "gleeful" about the imminent possibility of its demise, as it causes financial hardship to all. Politically speaking however, if it lessens the grip of undemocratic power currently being wielded against member states by Brussels, then its demise is welcome- and it is in everyone's interests, both in this country and on the continent, that it does not survive.

Yours,

(for freedom and democracy)

PS. Roland Rudd is related to the Tory MP Amber Rudd, as brother to sister:

Amber is one of four siblings, whilst the PR executive Roland Rudd, is a Labour supporter and donor advising Ed Miliband on business. The sister had the good sense to have divorced A.A Gill, but once shared his heart. That former family member and alcoholic writer who described the English as "embarrassing" and "an ugly race" who were "lumpen, louty, coarse, unsubtle, beady eyed" and a "beef bummed herd". He made further insulting remarks about the Welsh. Good to know that these people who are all intimately linked have the best interests of the British people and this country at heart.

On the death of Vaclav Havel (18th December 2011).

A great writer and a champion of democracy. His passing is a great loss. It also highlights the hypocrisy of the media with their fake "we are not like the USSR" propaganda message. A message spun on the BBC airwaves today. Indeed, for how can we claim we live in a post-communist, non-totalitarian, free and fair democratic Europe, when the EU is only a few steps away from being like the former USSR itself? Why, then, do we even now take increasing steps towards greater unity with this undemocratic, federal state? An organisation which endangers and imprisons the economies of individual countries within a single currency, and all for the sake of a political construct?

Our signing to the Lisbon Treaty without a referendum, and its refusal to accept the No vote from such countries as Ireland, are themselves damning indictments of EU's tyrannical agenda. How then can our PM claim he stands up for British interests in Europe, whilst he continues to cling to this federal debacle? Why does he justify a phantom veto whilst allowing the arranging of a Fiscal Compact intergovernmentally? Why does he continue to refuse a referendum with an exit question? We should not even be communicating with this unelected, corrupt Commission of bureaucrats. They instruct a Parliament as to legislation they appear to have no proper powers to legislate or repeal. We fool ourselves if we even think it is developing towards a democratic United States of Europe. How can it be even a USE when the President isn't even elected by the people in a free and open election? It is the very antithesis of constitutional rule with its legislation imposed by a cabal against the will of the people. We will need a lot more Vaclav Havel's before we are through untwining ourselves from the imminent, growing, and very real threat of the EU, which even now is turning into a totalitarian tyranny in our midst.

Yours
(for freedom and democracy)
Steven Parris Ward.

On listening to a BBC programme tracing the history of the EU on Radio 4 and going back to the '20s and '30s: December 22nd 2011.

It is the imposition of the will of a political elite, bolstered by the greed of a minority of plutocrats, rather than the will of the common people, that so often causes war and conflict. History shows that it has never been the common folk of Europe that started the wars. Indeed, had these good people been given a choice, the wars would never have occurred. In this respect, it has always been the politicians and plutocrats who have caused war, as they sought to increase their greater share of the power structure.

This is an irony particularly in respect of the EU; where the fear of war has so often been a method used to justify a strengthening of the elites' grip on state power. War is brandished in order to justify the subjugation of the will of the people. Peace is the elite's justification for more power. In this, it is an irony further compounded by the recent civil unrest which is occurring across the continent, due to the EU's increasingly imposed dictatorial austerity programmes.

The dream of the EU is a political dream, forged, it is claimed, by the will of the people and for the good of all, but one which clearly exists purely by political will, and for the perpetuation of a small bureaucratic oligarchy/ plutocracy, against the desires and interests of the majority. It is perpetuated by pseudo political idealism, which in reality is nothing more than a mask to hide the selfish desire of a political elite to extend their wealth and power in the face of common suffering.

To achieve their aims the EU utilises the masses for taxation and control without due representation. It masquerades as a democratic people's parliament, yet such a parliament has no power to legislate over and above the will of the European Commission: that cabal of bureaucrats who exist by virtue of no true democratic process. The remaining undesirables themselves even now appear to have been purged of power, subject as they are to the elite cabal which is now known as "The Frankfurt Group".

The EU has been perpetuated due to selfish motives for power and greed, as well as due to the politician's distrust of the capability of the masses. Such overriding distrust has led to a rejection by politicians of the true democratic process. It is a tyranny: the rejection of completed referenda that opposes its political will in such countries as Ireland is proof alone of that.

From the people's dream of a "community of nations trading peacefully", which has led to so much power being ceded by sovereign nations and Republics, has arisen a nightmare: the greatest betrayal of the will of the people, and the greatest erosion of western democracy the world has seen since Stalin. It stands today as the EU, which has taken on all the trappings of a Soviet state. It consists of an unelected Politburo called the European Commission, and an unelected President, a former Maoist Communist himself. It has, in collaboration with that unelected cabal the Frankfurt Group, removed elected rulers to replace them with EU technocrats sympathetic to their aims. These technocrats, who are determined as "experts" by the EU leaders, and who acquiesce to its demands to preserve and protect its federalist agenda, also have no true democratic mandate.

It is the hubris of politicians, their own distrust and greed (along with in some sad instances a misplaced idealism) which is destroying democracy in practise. It is, therefore, a damning indictment that the BBC (a public broadcasting service, and one paid for by the people as a public service) now seeks to perpetuate a biased campaign of support for such a corrupt, undemocratic system of government. This is in the face of public distaste, and in spite of virile opposition.

The BBC, one presumes, does not lack the intellect acumen to understand that the EU (an emerging Federal State) is tantamount to a destruction of the democracy of sovereign nationhood. Yet it appears not to care. Its biased agenda is a direct threat to the freedom of democratic citizenship that has been afforded to the people of Britain for centuries. Its success, ironically, is based on the presumption by the masses for many decades that it speaks always for the best interests of the people of Britain "to educate and inform". It has received this blessing largely held on trust before and during the war. This in spite of its pro- Nazi bias by its Director General Lord Reith; revealed in his writings, and put into practise through the blocking of Churchill's speeches from its airwaves preceding the war.

Today, in the BBC's support of the EU, it displays a profoundly anti-democratic and treasonous message, which champions a left wing /Communist agenda of federal, centralised, pro EU state government. It is a message at odds with the true spirit of what is British sovereignty and democracy. In its pro EU message, it displays scant impartiality. Neither does it truthfully represent the will of the majority, who largely despise EU's anti-democratic form of control. In the taxation of its supposed audience by force, in spite of many loathing its biased propaganda message, it reflects unsurprisingly the EU method of governance and taxation without representation. It claims to speak for the people, as do the politicians of the three main parties, but in reality it is essentially supportive of an ardent Europhilia. A biased passion that fails to represent impartially, and in doing so robs the majority of its true voice. Its impartiality is further undermined by the financing grants afforded to it by the European Union itself.

Yours
(for freedom and democracy)
Steven Parris Ward.

In response to a slur on the British Monarch and the charge of elitism.

There has been no more loyal and dedicated servant subject to the service of the people of this country than Her Majesty the Queen. A monarch that, though lacking her own political power, yet delimits the potential for politicians to become tyrants or dictators.

In respect to this, Monarchy does not equal less democracy, as Republicans would have us believe. Monarchy, rather, equals the limitation of politicians to impose absolute dictatorial power. This was the chief reason why Cromwell was executed and a King justly restored to the throne. The Queen's chief shortcoming, however, has been her gross underestimation of the power of EU legislation, and its move towards a federal state tyranny. A move which has largely made her power to delimit impotent. A move which has transformed a sovereign of Royal heritage into a mere citizen of the EU. A development which through her acquiescence to legislation presented before her, has largely been accepted by her own approval.

Yours

(for freedom and democracy)

Steven Parris Ward.

On Daniel Hannan's supposed Euroscepticism.

Thank you Mr Hannan for acknowledging UKIP's Nigel Farage, and his increasing popularity and gains in the polls. A generous act. I think as a member of your Euro constituency however I shall certainly be voting for UKIP and not the Liberal Tory party. The reason is your continued failure to explain to the public at large exactly why you (a so called "Euro-sceptic") continue to support a Conservative government that is clearly pro EU in its agenda and which, it appears, has every intention of following a strategy of remaining within it. Are there Conservative policies you consider override your Euro-scepticism? Is that not a rather odd position to be in for an MEP Euro-sceptic that has made it the very be all and end all of his cause?

That it is Cabinet policy for the Conservatives to be pro EU is clear- for how else can David Cameron justify his avoidance of an in/out referendum whilst continuing to say he is a sceptic? His scepticism is an oxymoron when he states he also wishes "to be a chief player in Europe and at the centre of Europe". It is a contradiction in terms by Cameron, and is based on a desire for the EU to be like the old EEC. It presupposes a naive assumption by him that a federal EU will accept national parliamentary power in preference to its centralised Commission's dictates. As a federal bloc, with an undemocratic Commission, such an assumption makes any future repatriation of powers appear increasingly unlikely after 2014, particularly under present Lisbon treaty rulings, and the approaching QMV.

Concerning your good self, I also do not understand why you accepted the candidacy of Barroso for President of the European Commission. Your support of this undemocratically "elected" former Maoist Communist, who is hell bent on destroying national sovereignties, centralising financial powers, denuding our British Parliament's powers of fiscal and legal decision making, appears frankly unpatriotic and hypocritical. Perhaps it is just plain misguided. I have yet to determine which.

One thing is clear, a Conservative "Euro-sceptic" of the Cameron persuasion is a stance which ensures he is no champion of "British interests", but provides only an abrogation of his duty to protect national state democracy. Such a position leaves open the door for usurpation by a federal tyranny.

I am also at a loss to understand how you, a supposed "sceptic", can support the campaign to allow Turkey to enter the EU, whilst you simultaneously have claimed in the past you wish the UK to leave the EU and renegotiate under EFTA. It now appears you support a Cameron position: an In with a repatriation of powers- an In/In referendum. Yet this is no more than a mere fake plebiscite, and no real choice.

Bearing this in mind, the more conspiratorially minded might even assume you are no more than a pro EU Conservative placeman. A shill, designed to split the UKIP vote. A foil to dilute the popular impact of an in/out campaign. A traitor to the cause of British democracy.

Yours

(for freedom and democracy)

Steven Parris Ward

1981 files: Lord Howe rejects as 'inconsiderate' comments on the managed decline of Liverpool.

The outrage is justifiable from some concerning this issue, but the emphasis on a North South divide should be viewed as self-defeating. Don't be fooled; for there is usually a strategy of divide and conquer at work here, and one senses darker forces at play also that might be pleased at such a result. It might further their wish to weaken a growing anti EU movement. The release of this information serves well to promote political bickering at a national level about the past, and distracts our awareness of the increasingly present danger: federalisation and cabal rule at the Continental level.

A federalisation strategy by the EU has promoted asset stripping to lessen the UK's economic power in preparation for the euro. It now seeks to reduce our military strength as a sovereign nation and as independent power in preparation for an EU military (e.g. the possible BAE-EADS merger). All this disguised in the name of a principle of openness and fairness to engage in a competitive "European" market. This rule of law has enabled British manufacturing and industry to be shackled, and the contracts our governments should have favoured and preferred on the national level to be over-ridden at a cost to British money and jobs.

Let it be clear, there has been a "managed decline" over successive decades all over the country since joining the EU, and yes I include even boroughs of London once filled with British based small businesses in that calculation. It would seem inevitable that a federal power centre would seek to asset strip a former superpower's industrial base first, and Liverpool's Cammell Lairds stood as that key base, with its superb ship building for the greatest navy in the world.

The question therefore arises should free market privatisation be favoured or nationalisation? It is clear, as with many things, that both should have existed in cooperation with an understanding of what was in the national interest. The decisions made should always consider the extent to which free enterprise is compatible with national security and national autonomy, as well a factors both political and economic. The barometer of that should not have been the efficacy of pure enterprise in a free market for pure profitability, an approach laudable, but essentially easily subverted to corporate greed, nor a system that merely strengthens and centralises the totalitarian power of the State, but more a blend of the two, dependent on the utilities and requirements for the good of the people.

Furthermore, the rest is a mere distraction. It is doubtful that a man of Lord Howe's personality would have had a "blazing row" with Heseltine in any instance based on his quiet demeanour and their shared pro EU stance. Their unity against Thatcher is well known, but old history. A cause of her demise and the last obstacle to any serious strident Euro-scepticism by anyone in serious political office, barring of course Nigel Farage.

One senses the growth of our troubles and the planned erosion of our nation as an independent power much more palpably since the time we joined ERM, and then EU. It has been proceeding swiftly in all areas of industry, commerce, economics, education and especially political office ever since. It has seen the decline of democratic accountability, an increased pressure to comply with European law, as well as an increased pressure to comply with EC governance. When we object we are reviled and blamed for not being a member of the euro; as if freedom of currency is a crime that negates the right to democratic decision making.

Perhaps too, the evidence that there has been something of a Thatcher revival, at least via UKIP, adds to the concern from EU HQ and their UK based minions that naturally would seek to dampen any EU scepticism. A scepticism which she once championed. It serves well to awake old in fighting by conveniently seeking to blame a woman who once stood as one of the few champions against their cause. Her later days as PM stood as a testament to the most passionate defence of British democracy, freedom and sovereignty this country has known since Winston Churchill. Unfortunately, as so many that have opposed Communist inspired dictatorships have discovered in the past, politicians can often find themselves surrounded by traitors to the cause of the good, whilst they plot in the background. In this respect, Thatcher failed, unlike Stalin, to keep her friends close, but her enemies closer.

Yours

(for freedom and democracy)

Steven Parris Ward.

http://www.youtube.com/watch?v=r14Dq3JFGkc

http://www.youtube.com/watch?v=wkRwMFy0CVM

http://www.youtube.com/watch?v=mFUn4heWAk8

The EU's Cultural Marxist agenda.

The EU is adopting the strategies of Cultural Marxism. It seeks to obliterate any notions of British history and national identity gleaned from its past as irrelevant and archaic. It brands patriots as "xenophobic", "nationalist", "populist" and "a danger". It seeks to rebrand British sovereignty and our national history as something corrupt and evil. It is re-educating our children to its cause by encouraging schools to forget the past and our great and noble traditions. It seeks to invoke a feeling of shame for once great national achievements of which the citizens should be proud. This concern for historical revisionism mimics the former Soviet Union; any great cultural achievements are being wiped clean from this generation's consciousness, and all in the name of European collectivism. They are being enforced through the ideology of Political Correctness and Critical Theory.

https://www.youtube.com/watch?v=gIdBuK7_g3M

https://www.youtube.com/watch?v=2ULJEgr6Fa8

Yours
(for freedom and democracy)
Steven Parris Ward.

In defence of capitalism, the most virtuous economic system yet devised- responding to Daniel Hannan, Telegraph (19th January 2012).

Personally, I do not tend to accept that free markets are inherently good or bad, moral or immoral; as they are driven only with the notion of profitability and not altruism, or morality, to ensure continuing success. In this sense, surely it is not the economic model, but the actions of the agent and what they do with these profits, for the benefit or detriment of others, that should determine whether they are deemed good or bad.

Ultimately, both free enterprise capitalism and state capitalism (the striving to communism), leads without ethical responsibility and guidelines to the same end: exploitation by an elite plutocracy of the poorer and by definition weaker (be it individual workers or businesses). This is achieved either by international corporations acting to capture the market as a monopoly or via the autocracy of State control. Accepting as one does the need to prevent this, or at least offset it, Capitalism and the free market appears an improvement as ideally it generates more wealth and profitability through competitiveness for all, but without ethical responsibility the end result appears to be identical to State capitalism (communism). One hopes however it is not simply the notion of fascism: that "the strong by nature must rule the weak" that determines this. One hopes human nature is not inherently exploitative, and must therefore undermine freedom through dictatorial control because "it is natural".

It is the implementation of ethical capitalism that Mr Cameron and Mr Osborne now seek to address after too much freedom in business and banking practise. To this end, education of good business practise and government guidance without sacrificing growth and profitability in a free market of private businesses is a tricky and difficult formula to judge. Increased legislation for transparency and accountability must be the order of the day, without undermining competitiveness. A culture of bonuses cannot be simply limited to the detriment of the City being closed to business.

In any case, it surely cannot be that property ownership, or a particular economic model, is inherently guaranteed to produce altruistic behaviour, or moral business practise or actions. Your point, I believe , is that capitalism and free contracts are superior to Socialism as an economic model. That they enhance moral decision making to an extent that does not suppose exploitation of others for profitability. This is because they are based on a notion of greater improvement for oneself and for others. Something guaranteed by the contract itself and the market itself. You presuppose that Socialism has no right to utilise tax payers money, as it is not theirs to do so, as it is in the hands not of free entrepreneurs, but is under State control, thereby encouraging favouritism and corruption. Free market capitalism is therefore good and state controlled nationalisation bad.

The above was the kind of libertarian economic model favoured by Milton Friedman. A view advocating less government and more liberty in private enterprise, ideally on the individual level. It is the individual who will ensure through the empowerment of profit that the monopoly will be curbed. I wonder however, what the role of government expenditure should be in such a free market scenario when a bonus culture amongst private companies has run riot for an elite few fat cats? Further, how is government to justify sanctions upon such individuals? Is this not hypocritical when they too allocate excessive funds and pay fraudulent expenses of the taxpayer's monies to themselves?

How in a free market is a private business supposed to apply ethics to their concern for profitability, when they are indeed free to act within extremely broad perimeters of ethical practise within a competitive market? The relationship here between governments and the businesses appears at best blurred by corruption, and the old adage "You scratch my back and I'll scratch yours" appears to be accepted. There appears in this respect anyway too much pork barrel spending and financing with vested interests.

I would like to think a solution could be found. To my mind an increase in legislation by government might well ensure ethical business practise. Yet this is not enough to guarantee profit accountability. Nor is it enough to ease the burden for those who feel exploited by such measures in the lower strata, or for those that feel it is unjust as they contribute to that business success, feeling as they do that they should be rewarded as much as possible. Indeed, the lower workers in a bonus culture, might feel marginalised and exploited by such rewards amongst the elite. The sweetening pill of awarding bonuses for future wealth creation of new businesses is a bitter pill to swallow when an increasing number appear less likely to contribute with new business ventures, dulled as they appear to have been by the excessive rewards they have unjustly and disproportionately been given.

To ensure less exploitation, surely the John Lewis model of enterprise and profit accountability should be encouraged for workers in partnership of firms. Energy companies too must readily enable a greater number of shares to be available for purchase on the markets for citizens who contribute to maintaining profitability of a company. Something more publicised by Thatcher, and which softened the distrust some felt for privatisation after years of nationalisation. There must be less presumption of fat cat salaries which are not based on performance, and an underlying ethic of profit sharing, with more visible and accountable transparency in improvement of services.

Yours
(for freedom and democracy)
Steven Parris Ward

On Napoleon and the building of a theme park in his honour; Telegraph (Jan 15th 2012).

Those that admired him invariably changed their minds when it became clear he was a tyrant and dictator, rather than a liberating visionary. Beethoven was typical of many whose opinion of him changed. The passage of time has blurred or blunted opinion. However, this new project to build a theme park in France is the equivalent of paying homage to a man comparable with Hitler. A warmonger, who was responsible for killing 2.5 million people. If anything it awakens a sense of patriotism and pride in Wellington's achievement (along with plenty of Prussian help), and the spirit of freedom inherent in British democracy. That a French minister deems him worthy of a theme park as a cause celebre says a lot for his misguided sense of what is honourable.

Yours

(for freedom and democracy)

Steven Parris Ward.

On Barack Obama and his ability and vision for "change": Jan 22nd 2012.

Obama is a great speaker. He has great speech writers. During the last campaign I (like most people) was really impressed with his ability to move with rhetoric. I warmed to his unity message of "Change you can believe in". There was an ability to channel Luther King, or an imagined Abe Lincoln. There was a sense of history in the making. That voice appealed to many Americans who wanted to feel proud, and not ashamed of their President; especially after an inarticulate Bush.

I did notice a good deal of disparity however between this moving, uplifting, dynamic Obama and the woolly headed, stuttering Obama in interviews. The latter appeared at best academic and dry, and at worst incompetent and vaguely mentally confused. His statements that he was unable to comment on certain issues because they were: "beyond my pay check" were worrying. He made a similar statement in visiting the EU when he claimed EU politics and economics were "confusing". In spite of his numerous ceremonial gaffes (still ongoing) overall his emotive speeches win the day.

Concerning his own politics he appears actually quite assured and not confused. He has confessed in his bio "Dreams of my Father" his fascination with Marxism and Socialism. He has also flirted with Marxist extremists in his early days: Bill Ayres, the terrorist from the 70's, now a college Professor, and Marxists of various types, such as Frank Marshall Davis and Alice Palmer, and particularly in his visits to Kenya and during his Chicago days. He has been influenced by the critical theory of Derrick Bell at University. His father and mother (a big influence) were respectively Communist and "Progressive" in their ideologies.

He should, therefore, not find the EU model quite as confusing as he states. Perhaps, however, he was merely noting the excessive use of bureaucracy and the lack of democratic accountability in his remarks on the EU. Characteristics typical of bureaucratic regimes that are concerned not with solutions, but with justifying their own importance and existence.

Now evinced in his policies, however, are the traces of this Socialist approach in his Federal centred Health and Police policies. These are a true indicator of an increase in more centralised control. Note- this President claims to be an expert on the Constitution, but criticises Congress for not 'getting things done'. This really means 'not doing as he says' quickly enough, in spite of that inhibition of presidential power being more constitutional.

Yet unlike Barroso- and our other President of the European Council - he has at least been elected by the people. Although, like them, he is a President ruling through Executive Orders: using 'Czars'- passing regulations through unelected government agencies padded with political appointees- and effectively run by recess appointments. This is a situation more akin to a king with courtiers ruling, than constitutional government. Since these policies and strategies have been tried in Europe, with disastrous consequences for sovereignty, freedom and democratic accountability, many feel he represents a real danger not just for US economic growth, but more importantly US democracy period.

Concerning the economy, he got off to a bad start in 2008. To rectify this, his State of the Union Address spoke about the banking crash. "The house of cards collapsed," he stated. "We learned that mortgages had been sold to people who couldn't afford or understand them." He criticised the banks that had "made huge bets and bonuses with other people's money", whilst "regulators looked the other way and didn't have the authority to stop the bad behaviour". Obama claimed this "was wrong". It was "irresponsible" and "it plunged our economy into a crisis".

Yet as an emerging politician in 1995, Obama was one of the chief campaigners for an amendment to the US Community Reinvestment Act. An Act that legally required banks to lend huge sums to millions of poor, mainly black Americans; guaranteed by the two giant mortgage associations- Fannie Mae and Freddie Mac. It was this Act, above all, which let the US housing bubble inflate beyond the point of safety. Due to this, hundreds of thousands of homeowners were faced with default. Furthermore, in 2005, no one more actively opposed moves to halt these reckless guarantees than Senator Obama himself, who received more donations from Fannie Mae than any other US politician.

Concerning democracy Obama is I believe either intelligent or stupid. As he graduated in Law and made a lot of money quickly, rising from relative obscurity, I surmise he isn't stupid. I wonder then why he appears so myopic concerning the undemocratic nature of the EU- an emerging Soviet style super state? Why is he unconcerned that it is changing into a new and very undemocratic Soviet style bloc? Why does it appear he is pressing on with a similar agenda in the US with NATU and increased federalisation?

I think the answer is clear: he is still effectively a Marxist in ideology and sympathies. A stance strengthened by his admiration of Saul Alinsky- the founder of Community Organisers in Chicago, Illinois- a Cultural Marxist and radical with covert Marxist sympathies in respect to his views on property rights.

Obama's policies are essentially driven by his ideology and political experience as a Community Organiser. His approach as President is to take these CO principles and apply them writ large. It need come as no surprise therefore that his politics is that of a Socialist- or more broadly- a Marxist. Indeed, his ideology is one informed by The Rules for Radicals approach of Alinsky; a man whom Obama has on a number of occasions claimed he was an admirer of.

However, Alinsky was more than a socialist, he was an anarchist, and was therefore a radical contemptuous of American materialism and individualism. Mindful of his need for covert agitation, he publically only referred to Lenin as a "pragmatist." In the context of his own approach to enacting radical methedology it is a term that damns Alinsky through faint praise.

Alinsky's idea of a new "vanguard" of suit and tie radicals operating covertly behind enemy lines was fulfilled to the highest specification with Obama's election as President. His approach has been to effectively change the system by "working in the system" — a

20

more effective approach for subversion than overt demonstration. In this, more profound results can be achieved through not acting or looking too radical. This in effect was so the populace wouldn't be unduly alarmed at any emerging radicalism.

Obama was first trained in Alinsky's rules in the 1980s, when radicals with the Chicago-based Alinsky group the Gamaliel Foundation recruited, hired, trained and paid for him to be a Community Organiser. They also helped him get into Harvard Law School by writing a letter of recommendation for him. During his Harvard years, Obama once took a break from his studies to travel to Los Angeles for eight days of training at Alinsky's Industrial Areas Foundation. In turn, he then trained other Community Organisers in Alinsky agitation tactics.

During the presidential campaign, he hired one Mike Kruglik, a Gemaliel mentor, to train young campaign workers in Alinsky tactics at "Camp Obama". This was centred at Obama headquarters in Chicago. The tactics helped Obama capture the youth vote impressively. After the election, his other Gamaliel mentor, Jerry Kellman, who hired him, helped the Obama administration establish "Organizing for America": a group movement which trains young supporters to agitate for Obama's legislative agenda using "Rules for Radicals" techniques.

Obama's strategy is also to seek "change" through the strategies of collectivism. This is achieved through increased federal power. He does, in this approach, appear to be emphasising the need for a NATU strategy. Such a strategy marks the beginning of a trade bloc that may develop, like the EU did in its earlier days, into a union which destroys freedom and democracy. Is this the sense of his new idea of a "greater union" ? It appears to be a euphemism, not for a more constitutional and economically successful USA union of member states, one which has flourished by virtue of its constitutional lessening of federal power and free market capitalism, but a trade bloc that paves the way towards a more centralised, authoritarian political bloc; a precursor perhaps to a future one world government.

Concerning his Marxist interests, he has been called the politically acceptable face of that, at least in Europe, as a "Socialist". A word still distrusted in America by the anti-Communist John Birch Society and the Republicans, as it is viewed as simply the economic, cultural and political face of Communism. A kind of "Communism lite". He is certainly at heart probably the most Socialist President the USA has ever had . Similar to Blair in his slick PR, he gives the public soaring rhetoric about equality for all and a sense of freedom. Yet he increases centralised control and a dependency on federal expenditure in seeming preparation for tougher times ahead. He speaks disparagingly of the rich, whilst suggesting campaign plans to tax them disproportionately. In this he incites class divisions, and displays the hallmarks of a true agitator. All this whilst he speaks of cooperation with Communist countries because "we cant make it on our own". He mixes this with the heady idealism of a future utopia.

In any case, the end result of any agreement to further NATU will be a political union, as the EU is attempting now. That realised EU model to date appears to care nought for democracy, and only for the implementation of an oligarchic/plutocratic dictatorial system of rule. It is a model of rule for enhancing greater, less democratically accountable centralised control.

In Obama's case, certainly his increased executive rule has represented a direct threat to the position of President as outlined in the US constitution. As Blair attacked the sovereignty in Britain, increasing EU political power whilst reducing the power of Westminster and the Queen, so Obama would like to reform the constitution of the USA, facilitating "a more perfect union" outside of the constitutional mandate with a more federal orientated agenda.

As a model to be imitated, it is the European notion of political progression Obama seeks to imitate. It is a trend towards collectivism, which negates any notions of individual achievement, personal betterment and national identity. The "international community" of politicians and oligarchs claim it is different from the old models; disguising its democratic deficits with the mask of corporate success, they speak of it in terms of "free market Capitalism", but it is in truth emerging as corporate fascism. They undermine individualism and free market enterprise for small businesses. Meanwhile, bureaucratic rulers enslave the populace with the facade of ideological egalitarianism, open borders and freedom for all- flooding countries with immigrants. Such open borders, which facilitate multiculturalism, erases national identity and culture. It in truth sows the seed for future civil unrest.

The reality, both politically and socially, is that a new emerging Federal State in Europe is just as tyrannic and dangerous as the old regimes of Communism or Fascism. First they claim it is merely a trade agreement. Then it becomes a political union. Next both the rich and the poor are laid low in the name of egalitarianism. Then you will be made to sing a new anthem and wave a new flag, as you are told that it isn't necessary to have the freedom to vote; for "work and compliance in itself brings freedom". Thence you are told "national patriotism is an archaic and dangerously xenophobic mode of thought". Everything will be decided by the perpetrators of the crisis originally (the self ordained plutocrats and technocrats) and to love and accept the New Order is and must be viewed as being in your true and best interests.

http://www.youtube.com/watch?v=pQtwo8lp_E8&feature=related

http://www.youtube.com/watch?v=2ANINZ8psz4&feature=related

http://www.youtube.com/watch?v=SyAgQJk4q5c&feature=related

http://www.youtube.com/watch?v=3KzKor5s6r8

Yours
(for freedom and democracy)
Steven Parris Ward.

On the FOI disclosure request by the BBC for Royal Honours (24th Jan 2012).

Not all honours rejections are a snub. Consider as an example Hughie Green. He was an ardent Monarchist. He also believed Harold Wilson was a covert Communist and Prince Philip would be better suited as PM. He refused an OBE in the 1960s because he considered himself "not worthy".

What is the purpose in this disclosure of information? The FOI act was requested on behalf of the BBC. The BBC: an organisation that champions some of the key issues of Cultural Marxism via its propaganda regime, in the furtherance of a pro EU agenda.

The purpose of this request appears to be to sully the prestige of such awards and the current government, attack the Monarchy, and champion further the idea of a Republic.

I personally do not find the idea of a Republic unacceptable in a country confident in its independent political power, the autonomy of its Justice system and Courts, and its sovereignty to enact decision making (both economic and judicial) through democratically elected representatives. When, however, it is increasingly apparent that the UK is becoming no more than a vassal state of the EU, one wonders whether figureheads such as the Queen should be abandoned when she prevents, by her existence, the growing move towards greater political integration with this corrupt, undemocratic monolith of Communist leanings.

A figurehead whose prime purpose in its reinstatement was to prevent Political leaders such as Cromwell from assuming absolute dictatorial power has, whatever its shortcomings and faults, served to protect and delimit the power of tyrants against the people. Substitute Barroso and his Commissars for said unelected dictators who seek further integration and political control against the democratic will of the people.

Yours
(for freedom and democracy)
Steven Parris Ward.

Should the Germans stop being German?: 26th Jan 2012.

One of the characteristics of the Germans is they never give up. Inherent within their national psyche is unfortunately their inability to deviate from any planned course of action once they have embarked upon it. The U turn so beloved by the British is not one of their capabilities. This was demonstrated by their inability to accept surrender during the Second World War, even when it was apparent that Berlin was decimated. This quality, however, serves them well in competitive football matches. Whether it works in the bendy realm of Real Politik is less clear.

Concerning the EU crisis, I expect them to continue seeking every means at their disposal to keep the euro alive. They will do this by hoodwinking others into paying for the firewall and bailouts. Meanwhile, they will steadfastly refuse to further add to bail out funds themselves, so they can benefit from a low euro and competitive exports. They will refuse to make the Deutsche E.C.B. the endangered bank of last resort, thus maintaining fear in the markets. Simultaneous, they will doggedly forge ahead with political union, which in effect means the rule of Europe via Brussels and the Reichstag. A scenario of idealism which ironically might well oversee the dissipation of Germany as an independent self-governing nation. In the long term it could yield only an acquiescence to a Communist, collectivist style of rule, maintained with an autocratic hegemony, developed by virtue of the EU Commission. The subservience of former countries will be attempted through increasing austerity until total control is ensured.

To avoid such a bleak future scenario, Mr Cameron must summon up the one U turn that really matters to the British people and transform himself into a hero: this being the restoration of UK Independence by leaving the EU. An alternative scenario could be that as the realisation by Germany that they cannot continue to support poorer member states begins to dawn, they will return to the Deutsche Mark, or a collapse of the Eurozone will ensure a euro currency traded by a small core of affluent states. The repatriation of gold by the Bundesbank from the Federal Reserve signifies a possible return to the gold standard.

(for freedom and democracy)

Steven Parris Ward.

"Commentators sometimes talk of the EU as having been constructed on 'Cartesian' lines, meaning that it was designed in the logical French tradition rather than the empirical British one.", Daily Telegraph (28th Jan 2012).

Dear Mr. Hannan,

The Euro is not based on the French Cartesian model of "I think therefore I am", as opposed to the British Empirical model of "I think what I see", but rather Germanic Idealism. Yet in this they act truly Irish, as they cling to the Berkeleian maxim of "To be is to be perceived". For the Europhiles inhabit a world of concepts and ideas that they regard as substantive reality, when the reality is, as any clever rationalist will tell you, that they are groping around in the dark of a Platonic cave of economic and political fuddle. They are chasing no more than illusory shadows. Whether such Germanic Idealism will reveal itself in its inversion as true Marxism, only time will determine.

They reveal their ignorance with their rhetorical statements, as opposed to their actions based on knowledge, as most politicians do. A trait Plato famously noted. Add to that the further Socratic maxim that: " Only a fool thinks themselves truly wise", and they betray their inabilities at every meeting, speech and turn of the teleprompter.

Their only cure is a good dose of Realism and rational thinking, so that they can free their minds from the chains of their Europhilia illusions. They need to ascend into the light of the true reality, so they can face the truth. This being the admission that the euro is a failure, it stifles and eventually kills economic competition between member states, shackling differing GDP's under a single currency is doomed. Rationally they must return to base and restore original currencies. They can then devalue, understand the patterns of reason and logic, follow the currents of the changing markets, and adapt accordingly. They need to get a grip.

Yours,

(for freedom and democracy)

Steven Parris Ward.

On Cameron's U turn of the Veto: Telegraph, 30th January 2012.

Dear Mr Hannan,

If Mr Cameron represents the minority view in the Conservative party, as you claim, how can the PM continue to credibly lead the party? Are the Conservatives now being led, against the majority view, to act in ways that are clearly pro EU? Mr Cameron's fudged referendum promise and strategy for remaining within EU governance (via adherence to Lisbon Treaty rules) is clearly no more than a delaying tactic to further capitulation. Prevarication can only further the charge against him: that he leans towards a pro integrationist, one State agenda. If so, democracy in his own party appears to be a sham. They certainly cannot claim themselves to be united, if the majority oppose the PM's continued capitulation to Brussels.

The developments today add further to the feeling that we are witnessing a slow motion coup d' etat. A continued membership being justified by Cameron, he claims, for "British economic interests". A claim made consistently by successive leader's, when economic arguments prove the EU is in truth inhibiting our trade interests globally. Moreover, what price is to be had for Parliamentary democracy and sovereignty?

The public should demand a definition concerning his stance on Europe in clear and unequivocal terms. This should be met with an immediate and televised full public address. For example: what does he mean by "defending British interests in Europe"?; a vague notion at best. A notion that means different things dependent on the speaker being for or against membership. What is his definition of being a "Euro-sceptic"? His scepticism appears to contradict, as an oxymoron, his desire to be "at the heart" of EU decision making. He is continually ceding more powers to Brussels. He should, therefore, make a public speech addressing these deficits of logic; lest he be accused, and quite rightly so, of aiding and encouraging the erosion of British democracy and sovereignty. Charges that should invoke an immediate referendum, which if denied further should trigger the charge of malfeasance and treason.

Mr Cameron often talks about British interests in the EU and that he is a sceptic. His pre Christmas speech addressing the single market represented no more than a desire for an EEC now long superseded by an emerging and increasingly authoritarian EU Government. His sole emphasis on the single market appears only to be a rouse to fool the public. It is a PR balm- an unction- that he seeks to use to soothe the concerns of a public worried by increasing federalism and tyranny. It is a strategy that is not working. For the public are becoming more outraged by the governments' indecision to act to defend British sovereignty.

We are increasingly being controlled by an undemocratic cabal of unelected Eurocrats. These Eurocrats are pressuring nations via the Commission, Frankfurt Group and IMF into an undemocratic Federal State of Europe where autonomous fiscal and economic decision making is being unndermined.

It is clear there is only one party to vote for (failing a referendum by the Tories) and that is UKIP; if indeed, as the majority do, they want to leave the EU. Certainly the Socialist Collectivists that are Labour will not break free of the teat of their beloved Mother State, and the Liberal Democrats positively drool over their love relationship with Brussels- a compliant party easily controlled by the EU's unremitting agenda of political correctness.

Yours,

(for freedom and democracy)

Steven Parris Ward.

The influence of Communism on the Western mind: 30th Jan 2012.

To the Libertarians of Britain,

Most intellectuals, of different political persuasions, admit that the danger of totalitarianism is just as prevalent today as it was during the Cold War. Even under Putin, evidence has been released that the gulags have, contrary to popular opinion, still been maintained and not dismantled. People are demonstrating presently about the undemocratic nature of his so called "elections", which to all intents and purposes appear to be rigged and not representative of any true democratic process. The lack of human rights, and the shift to a more fundamental party approach in China is another current example.

Communism is inherently collectivist, and therefore an annihilator of the freewill of individualism. It seeks control for the interests of the State through autocratic, totalitarian control. The denial of individual free speech is a necessity if it opposes its interests. It is undemocratic and signifies the end of individual human rights and freedoms; the death of sovereign nations, the end of free market capitalism and market competitiveness.

By Communism I mean that totalitarian form of political rule brought about by the Soviets during the Cold War period (developed under tyrannical rule by Stalin and Lenin). I do not mean the utopian form to be achieved post Socialism as Marx indicates as his ideal when the state is no more. A utopia which appears to be unachievable in any case, without a total subjugation of democratic freedom and individualism. It requires any political regime that aspires to it to implement a tyrannical police state.

The current notion of collectivism, embodied in the undemocratic form of rule as championed by the European Commission for the Union, is to all intents and purposes moving towards the former Communist/ Soviet model of single state governance. It will be under the control of an E.U. Commission hegemony. This hegemony displays only the facade of democracy in the Parliament which has no power to independently legislate over the Commission. How or why has this come about?

With the defection of Golitsyn during the Cold War, it has formerly been claimed that global domination by the Soviet Union was sought with the implementation of Perestroika as a tactic of deception. A process designed to implement not true democratic reform in the USSR, but a process which marked the start of a covert Leninist strategy. It achieved this by "adopting the mask of the enemy". The strategy sought to effect political control of the West by stealth. It was to be achieved, according to Golitsyn, under the facade of accepting democratic change to the USSR bloc itself. In actuality, however, it sought hegemonic rule, via the infiltration of the EU via Marxist sympathisers; those favourable to the cause of Communism.

All this was to be achieved whilst Russia itself was maintained under fundamentally autocratic control. A situation which appears true under Putin, and the continuing maintenance of the KGB power cells and the Siberian gulags. The restoration of treason laws recently for improper political views against Russia, as well as the restoration of the Soviet national anthem, add further to the feelings of deceit.

The infiltration of European institutions, filled with Communist political sympathisers, utilising covert methods, has been achieved and developed unopposed. A possibility that would have been largely impossible during the espionage and surveillance of the Cold War. Such a claim might appear farcical, if it were not for the fact that such claims are supported by the progression of political events of history- the EU is also now supervised by many formerly ardent Communists, some though not all from former Soviet states themselves. Further, the activities of Common Purpose, at the community and council level, is indicative of ideological advocates who are independently sympathetic to the cause.

Concerning Golitsyn specifically, his predictions have been proven as fact, with over 94% of his predictions occurring. This percentage substantiates his claims that he was privy to the long term Soviet strategy for Western capitulation to Communism as a KGB Soviet agent. Predictions such as: the dismantling of the Berlin Wall, and the unification of East Germany with the West; the changing of the name of the KGB, whilst keeping its functions; the role of Gorbachev, etc. have all been proven correct.

The infiltration of the European Economic Community with former Soviet politicians and the "development" of the European Union is one result of this strategy it seems. The takeover of sovereign nations' democratic governance by pro EU autocrats, the imposition of austerity measures effected utilising economic subversion methods, these being achieved with the imposition of the euro, have been a logical progression of Golitsyn's claims.

The strategy involves "appearing weak"- a classic military strategy of Sun Tzu. Required reading in the former Soviet and East German military. Further planks to support the aim are: the global drug offensive; the war on terror offensive; the international criminal offensive and the Gramsci inspired Cultural Marxist strategy- essentially a covert strategy of culture attack.

In relation to Europe- the infiltration and building of a dictatorial, Communist inspired model, has already been effected and is continuing. The economic strategy has been brought about by the imposition of the Euro through the hegemony of the European Commission and its legislation. For example, it is now a necessity to join the Euro for new membership under Lisbon. This already presents an effective prison house for those nations in the present Eurozone. New countries will not be able to invoke article 50 of Lisbon legislation once obliged to join the euro. This treaty is most evidently undermining autonomous governmental control at the national level. The current euro crisis also signifies not the end of the euro, but the increase in drives towards a Federal State tyranny. This will continue to impair democratic accountability and economic decision making. Federal tyranny will be further strengthened via the EU's Troika and Frankfurt Group- in league with the politically biased and corrupt IMF- which is now controlling Greek and Italian parliaments with the imposition of unelected technocrats.

Even if it is disputed that this is not a deliberate covert plot, it appears the end achievement of the EU is still to develop towards a single state collective, and this by its nature is tantamount to a form of totalitarianism; a Soviet style tyranny of some kind. In this aim, it seeks to abolish sovereign political power in individual nations with the implementation of the ECHR and ECJ directives, which the EU now appears to be cannibalising. These override the will of national state governments and their courts. The latter provisions, to protect national democracies, are now virtually accepted as powerless in any case, at least within the legislation of the Euro Zone, and enforced specifically through the legislation of the Lisbon Treaty. The move to abolition of intergovernmental decision making and veto power adds to this impotency, and has been confirmed also by Barroso's recent State of the Union speech (2012).

Political Union without democratic accountability appears tantamount to a tyranny, irrespective of whether it is Soviet inspired or led. Certainly political union for the EU is a goal now openly discussed as the aim by many of the former political leaders of formerly Communist persuasion. Angela Merkel and Barroso are often cited by the media concerning their ambitions to ensure the EU develops, not simply as a single economic market, but as a greater political union. The aim is a single unified State entity. In this, both appear to be also accepting of legislation that suppresses national culture in favour of a common cultural emphasis. This is to develop the sense of the EU's notion of a European identity, or has been often termed in the EU friendly media: "a single country".

Irrespective of supposed Soviet strategy, the effects of Cultural Marxism on the UK, as well as in the USA, have been well documented. It has been implemented by Marxist sympathisers, be they Leninists, or of the Fabian and Frankfurt types. Their aim is to corrupt democratic societies, preparing them for a neo-Marxist approach to government. Such campaigns have been largely successful, but their aim will result not in a utopia, but only in a totalitarian form of rule enforced by a police state; as evinced by the history and deaths perpetrated by the former USSR, and evident in the atrocious human rights record of present day Communist China.

The subversion of western democracies is being achieved utilising the classical tactics of Fabius. These are designed to induce first a covert cultural and eventually economic and military revolution, via primarily peaceful methods, through a war of attrition waged incrementally. These have been notably outlined by the Frankfurt School and Fabians in Western Societies, as well as elucidated by Gramsci.

Disinformation and the implementation of junk values have been propagated for decades as a form of subversion. A campaign waged by the Marxists under the sanitised claim that Socialism is an acceptable form of political governance which strives for egalitarianism and peace, and does not aim towards collectivist, dictatorial, Communist rule accredited to it by history. Socialism is, however, in reality simply a stage once removed in the process towards one party state totalitarianism. It is the politically acceptable face of state control- a question of degree and nothing more- which seeks to achieve via similar economic tactics and cultural subversion the same state ruled collectivist end as Communism.

The approach ultimately seeks to undermine free enterprise capitalism and private property ownership, passing it into state hands. It seeks the destruction of small businesses through the implementing of greater red tape and bureaucracy, brought about through increased state power. Its inherently collectivist approach, utilises the fruits of free market capitalism to increase its governmental powers. Rather than promoting individualism and liberty as prime values both socially and economically. It seeks absolute egalitarianism with the notion of commonality of outcome, stifling and subjugating freedom of opportunity.

Unfortunately the EU, with its absorption of former Soviet countries, is well on the way to overtly assuming an unelected, undemocratic Socialist/ Communist face and control agenda. The proposition of a single army and military capability for the EU is also cause for great concern for the maintenance of peace. It adds to the building pressure to dismantle NATO. The development of such military might poses a direct threat to the future security of the United States.

The future New World Order, if succesful, will merely develop as an emerging of four chief zones. China with Korea, Japan and parts of South East Asia. Russia shall merge with the new European Union bloc with parts of Africa and the middle East. The US will merge with Mexico, Canada and further parts of Middle and South America. Australia will merge with South Asia, the Philippines, etc. The characteristics of some zones will be an undemocratic totalitarian, form of State rule. This form of rule will be enforced primarily by economic subversion. This will signal the death of national democracies, as well as the end of liberty and human rights as understood for the individual, as it only champions collectively what is in state interests of the oligarchy.

Future prospects for the United States to be incorporated within the NWO appear to be gaining momentum with the ongoing dismantling of its constitution, the centralisation of government, and an increase in its bureaucratic powers at the federal level. A currently Socialist/ Marxist leaning President furthers the agenda. The suggestion of a collectivist trade bloc known as the North American Trade Union will mark the beginning of a move to further political union and its merging with Canada and Mexico. The emergence of the Amero and greater monopolies will occur as a cause of this.

It is not yet possible to determine whether the future NAU will lack the democratic accountability that characterises the European Union as a political entity. The failure of it to abandon democratic representation will inevitably lead it into direct military conflict with the EU Communist bloc of the New World Order. It is possible that any attempt to subvert its constitution will inevitably lead to internal struggles and civil conflict in any case.

To achieve these ends the personality traits and characteristics of the Cultural Marxists in Britain who operate largely covertly are worth noting. They have until recently sought to achieve revolutionary change passively through covert and not military means. This however must be viewed as a precursor to violent agitation and military terrorism, which many have in the past championed and advocted. They reveal their radical fundamentalism in psychological traits which many might find objectionable, irrespective of political persuasion. These being:

1. A broad hatred, expressed vehemently, of the merits of free market capitalism. This is usually justified as a class struggle that champions the worker, and which exploits the notion of a rich/poor divide. This, however, in reality, ultimately exploits and subjugates the worker by robbing them of social mobility, increasing state dependency in many instances due to the minimum wage, limiting the money obtainable by individuals achieved through free enterprise to achieve higher standards, etc. All this is presented under the name of state governance to achieve a classless egalitarianism which in effect shackles the individual both socially and

fiscally. It further delimits their democratic power to elect change of rule as individuals through perpetuating the false consciousness of state dependency. This is maintained in the interest of maintaining the oligarchy and power structure of the State, ideally as a one party State government system, or if not one, a two or three party system with mutual sympathies. The method incorporates a classic strategy of divide and conquer to achieve their aims amongst the working and middle class.

2. A venomous hatred expressed against any form of Constitutional Monarchy, which they believe inhibits absolute state control and political power. Anarchists invariably portray themselves as Republicans championing their democratic rights as citizens, who despise the Queen, whilst simultaneously often inciting hatred generally against the prosperous, and those that, through their own industry and enterprise, have achieved financial independence.

3. A covert attempt via media organisations, expressed via hidden and sometimes disguised internet groups, to subvert institutions, cause confusion, and lessen the morale and belief of citizens in the value of such institutions. This is often centred against the people through detraction, distraction, belittlement and bombardment. This consists in wide ranging concerted attacks on any form of news or media via commentaries that support the bedrock of national unity and identity. The media, in producing controversial, nihilistic stories, are also, unwittingly or otherwise, part of this campaign. For example, attacks are often focused on the value of a country's literature, music and art. Also the value of its citizens, and their contribution to the world as a nation. Any justification to belittle national achievement on the world stage, as well as exceptional individual achievements identified with that country are often made.

Generally attacks on scientific or mechanical inventions via the media and blogs, that denote outstanding intellectual achievement are, often made. The strategy is to lessen pride and morale in one's country. There is also a broad concern with historical revisionism. This seeks to support notions of a country having had a "disreputable past" that promoted "immoral conduct", etc., and of which the present citizens should be ashamed.

4. The promotion of nihilism is a recurrent theme and strategem- also utilised in subverting the judicial system. This is achieved via support of terrorist figures, rewarding thieves, murderers and rapists, by championing the notion of their human rights, which are simultaneously removed from those victims of the crime, the citizens who abide in acceptable ways, many of whom are also punished severely for relatively minor transgressions.

5. The subversion of morals is utilised often through idealism or claims to be pacifist. The encouragement of the view that patriotism and pride for one's country is something of which the people should be ashamed, as it promotes archaic tribalism, and not progressive values that strive for peace. Peace is often expressed with a biased tendency favouring non opposition to the Communist ideology. Hence the waving of the national flag, or even displaying it, is tantamount to a display of excessive nationalism invoking the spectre of British fascism or British Imperialism which, they

claim, is best subjugated, as it leads to war. Such a repressive psychology, brandished under the banner of political correctness, has been recently apparent in Barroso's speeches. It is notable that the waving of national flags which are described as an act of "xenophobia" in displays of patriotic fervour, do not apply to the waving of the European flag.

6. The development of the Common Purpose network via councils, and other institutions, are responsible for the promotion of bad taste public art, and the lax attitude to the public desecration of war memorials whilst not repairing them. This is also achieved with the general misappropriation of funds to effectively improve or maintain local infra- structure. Common Purpose also oversees, via its trained agents in the councils, child abductions from those families or foster parents deemed politically incorrect; i.e. those parents who are not of a socialist or of a left wing political persuasion.

Yours,

(for freedom and democracy)

Steven Parris Ward.

http://www.youtube.com/watch?v=JhZHJhSjN8w

http://www.youtube.com/watch?v=y3qkf3bajd4&feature=related

http://www.youtube.com/watch?v=jt44D6ZlFKI

"J'accuse Mr Cameron"- written in response to the claim David Cameron is proud of Britain, its democracy and freedom. (Daily Telegraph 15th April 2012).

Dear Mr Cameron,

You sir are no Conservative. You are a "Progressive Liberal" at best, in league with promoting the undemocratic, collectivist agenda of the EU and its aim to fiscal and political union. A man who works to override British sovereignty and democracy, by promulgating the notion of continuing membership against the will of the majority of British people.

You are a politician who works with corrupt former Communists and members of the Supreme Soviet. You work with an unelected Maoist in the EU President Barroso. You lie to the people of Britain when you justify such institutions as democratic; for they are controlled without a democratically elected mandate. You sir are a "useful idiot", as Lenin might have termed it.

However, recognising your background as a Philosophy graduate from the institute of Oxford I fear the worst: that you are in truth no misguided fool, but a covert Cultural Marxist, who seeks to undermine the British economy, judicial system, religious institutions, family values, etc in such a manner as would have made Gramsci, Lenin and the Fabian Socialists proud.

Your agenda, in short, appears to be to undermine British cultural values, political and judicial institutions, the military and indeed the economy. Your strategy strengthens further EU meddling and integration. It poses a direct threat to British democracy. You are promoting the EU's ultimate end aim of a Federal State of Europe with your denial of a referendum, and a faux scepticism that campaigns for a fictitious repatriation of powers. Seventy five percent of our laws are now determined by Brussels. The absorption of Britain and its democracy into rule by an undemocratically elected tyranny appears to be at hand.

Below a list of the strategies that you and your cohorts have so far achieved to fulfil your objective to greater absorb Britain into the corrupt, non-democratic EU hegemony:

I charge you with the following treasonable offences against the British people, their democracy and freedom.

J' ACCUSE

Deliberate instruction to relax border controls for EU citizens. A covert instruction that supported the Schengen borderless agreement that Britain did not agree to become part of in the first place.

Facilitating employment and jobs to EU nationals in preference to British (London buses, Olympics, etc) without first approaching and or "proper" advertising of said vacancies in the British press, but advertising them in East European job centres.

Deliberate wasting of taxpayers resources to run down the economy. One example being the overseas aid programmes. In spite of billions being wasted, overseas aid barons paying themselves millions in contract bonuses- countries that received said funds making official statements that they "needed no such funds"- and some of these countries being currently rich, or Communist, undemocratic regimes, billions have continued to be wasted. This has been further compounded by simultaneous payment via both British and EU aid programmes, many of which have now been proven to be wasted scandalously on vanity projects in Barbados, South Africa, and on celebration parties for the Eurocrats themselves.

Welfare to Work: the selection of corrupt employment agencies, furnishing them with contracts that achieve nothing, whilst they siphon off millions in fake profits to line their own pockets. Many other examples of your cosy corrupt nepotism (Adrian Beecroft, cash for policies, Rebekka Brooks) are by now well known and unbefitting of a public servant and PM.

A phantom veto: used in order to avoid pre-election promises of a referendum if further treaties were ratified. You renege on your promise when the fiscal compact was in reality a new treaty by any other name according to your comrades the Hungarian Sarkozy and the former East German Socialist Angela Merkel. A fiscal compact that enforced further the steps towards political union in both Merkel and Sarkozy's opinions. A compact that overrides autonomous, economic decision making at the national level. You sought the veto to avoid a referendum, but then sought to arrange and support elements of the fiscal compact intergovernmentally.

Continuing to support ECHR, ECJ and EU legislation. This effectively nullifies British Justice and champions the rights of EU rapists, illegals, murderers and other criminals to reside and continue to remain in this country to commit further crime. In this context also you continue to support the denial of habeas corpus, and promote EU legislation, in order to further enhance the ability of extradition orders to be made against British citizens without a court or trail, or presentation of prima facie evidence to determine the justification of charges.

Dismantling the British armed forces whilst promoting the European taskforce. You have personally championed and campaigned for the BAE- EADS merger to effect this. You have also overseen a massive reduction in Army and Navy personnel in spite of our engagement in Afghanistan.

The destruction of the traditional nuclear family: effected with the blurring of traditional family values through a bias towards homosexual sex education to children via education programmes, and by the move towards outlawing the use of titles such as "husband" and "wife", amongst other measures. This is further achieved with the promotion of gay marriage in the name of political correctness. As well as perpetuating extortionate child care costs which further penalise mothers in their attempt to work. Further championed by the denial of separated fathers to visiting rights after separation from former spouse (claimed to preserve the family), whilst simultaneously you have sought to destroy the nuclear family by fiscal measures: Married couples with children who live on one earner's average income in Britain pay 73 per cent of the tax that a single person without children has to pay. CARE says that the government — that is, the system you are personally responsible for — "penalises stable couples and encourages family breakdown and un-partnered childbearing."

The vilification of traditional C of E believers with the outlawing of crosses and the right to pray at work during break time for public servants. I as a non- believer still support the rights of British Christians to practise their faith. You as a Christian should too, but by your prevarication and championing of said ECHR and politically driven vilifications and council pronouncements do not. Further your championing of same sex marriage in Church contravenes religious ideology as outlined in scripture. Civil ceremonies afford the same rights to same sex partnerships and should be sufficient. The majority of believers further find such same sex marriage ceremonies in church objectionable. Whilst the majority of the gay community profess a disinterest in the issue.

The following offences directly violate the office of PM to protect and serve the Crown and the British people- their democracy and freedom – being in direct violation of the ancient edicts of Magna Carta, the Bill of Rights and Common Law – as well as common British decency and justice. Virtues by which this country has been rightly hailed with her title "The Mother of Modern Democracy".

You remain ei incumbit probatio qui dicit, non qui negat as a British Citizen, until pronouncement and sentence is passed at the next election.

Yours,

(for freedom and democracy),

Steven Parris Ward.

In response to Tim Stanley's article (23rd April 2012) in the Daily Telegraph that Heath was not a foe of British democracy.

Dear Dr. Stanley,

Your profile indicates you are a supposed loyal, right wing, anti EU "Conservative", who was not born until the 1980's. It is not advisable, therefore, to try to persuade disenchanted voters that lived through it, that the deceitful Heath was really not such a bad guy after all. The reason for your support of the man who took Britain into the embryonic EU rests in your conclusion, where you state Mr. Heath acted as he did because he was just trying to keep the peace. An oft advocated justification for EU expansionism. A proviso you also appear to offer as a general pardon for Conservative politicians from successive generations, who can perhaps be excused for not doing their job properly, because, you claim, they were simply politicians of their time who were compromised from their true ideals by the "contemporary consensus".

In this you appear to want to suggest that it is not really the politician's that are at fault, but their need to be elected, and their pampering to the popular view once in power, that has largely caused the problems. I suggest however that it is quite the reverse; for politicians make promises to achieve the popular vote in their pre-election manifesto, only to back track on these promises after they have been elected. They do this due to the fact they have ideological convictions that they fear are, and indeed would be, unpopular. In this they are proven to be liars who flatter to deceive. Such is the case with the current bunch of turncoats, and such was the case with Edward Heath.

Heath was, however, not simply a product of his time, but a man whose whole life as a politician was set on justifying a lie. This is the man who justified the lie that joining the EEC would involve "no essential loss of British democracy and sovereignty" in the referendum campaign. A lie he then sought to justify in his twilight years by stating the standard EU rhetort:

"Well if you didn't want economic and political union, why did you vote Yes to join in the first place?"

It was only a few years after joining this that the true Conservative Enoch Powell, a British patriot effectively consigned by Heath to the political wilderness, bemoaned with a prescience befitting of a prophet:

"This is the first and last election at which the British people will be given the opportunity to decide whether their country is to remain a democratic nation, governed by the will of its own electorate, expressed in its own Parliament, or whether it will become one province in a new European super state, under institutions which know nothing of the political rights and liberties that we have so long taken for granted."

Those words Dr. Stanley are not simply a product of their time, nor do they need any apology or justification, as your revisionist argument would want to suggest. They require no justification as the errors of Heath do. Errors which have destroyed this once free and democratic nation. They are words reflective of a truly Conservative, democratic ideology; words more pertinent today than when they were first uttered.

Yours,

(for freedom and democracy)

Steven Parris Ward.

"There is no question of any erosion of essential national sovereignty."
"There are some in this country who fear that in going into Europe, we shall in some

way sacrifice independence and sovereignty. These fears I need hardly say are completely unjustified"
Ted Heath, British Conservative Prime Minister and noted Europhile. White Paper on the implications of joining the EEC, July 1971. Proven by later release of documents to be outright lies.

"There will not be a blueprint for a Federal Europe"
Ted Heath, British Conservative Prime Minister and noted Europhile. Speech in the House of Commons, 25 February 1970 in run-up to EEC entry.

"There is no danger of a single currency."
Ted Heath, British Conservative Prime Minister and noted Europhile. EEC membership information leaflet, 1975.

Sissons: "...the single currency, the United States of Europe: was that on your mind when you took Britain in?"
Heath: "Of course, Yes."
Ted Heath, British Conservative Prime Minister and noted europhile, and Peter Sissons, BBC journalist and presenter. Question Time with Peter Sissons, 1 November 1991.

On Hannan's supposed Euro-Scepticism, Telegraph, 3rd May 2012.

Dear Mr Hannan,

Sir, you quite rightly comment in respect of the EU that we have "shackled ourselves to a corpse". Perhaps then you can kindly explain why you continue to support The Friends of Turkey Campaign for EU expansion to add further to the bloating of this corrupt, infested corpse? Why also did you support the head of this corpse (Barroso) in his appointment as President in your role as a Conservative MEP? Should not the bloated corpse (the undead vampire so to speak) not have been decapitated, so it could rest in peace, and not seek to drain further economic life power and monetary blood from its victims?

With such actions Mr. Hannan you have acted only as a "useful idiot"; a Renfield in the service of the Prince of Darkness, rather than a hero of freedom and goodness. Daniel we want you to be a heroic Van Helsing, not a Renfield stooge!

Yours,

(for freedom and democracy)

Steven Parris Ward.

Europe's voters are in denial about the need for austerity; the solution is more democracy, Telegraph, 14th May 2012.

"One of the great comments on this issue, though it takes the form of subtext, comes in Robert Harris's Cicero novels. By any conventional measure, the hero of that late republican period was Cato. He was cited for centuries afterwards as a paragon of selfless virtue and political principle. His name was taken by several of the American patriot pamphleteers, as it had been by an earlier generation of English radicals. But Harris brilliantly portrays him as Cicero (or Peter Mandelson) would see him: as a self-obsessed nuisance, driven mad by an over-literal application of his logic to complex situations. That view of Cato is the authentic voice of the professional politician down the ages."

Dear Mr Hannan,

Unfortunately it is not the noble and virtuous Cato the Younger (Farage) whom we have in a position of authority, but Sulla (Barroso) and his informing head hunters (the Commissars). These people are the one's exerting control. With their millions they determine the insane narrative. The very type of dictator and corrupt cronies that Cato himself nobly fought against in rhetorical criticism, now determine how the voices of reason are defined.

Yet in spite of these ploys to slur, we have those very qualities ordained by the Senate that identify the dictator:

legibus faciendis et reipublicae constituendae causa.

I translate and identify his wickedness and corruption therefore with his undemocratically ordained role as dictator:

"for the making of laws and for the settling of the constitution". An epithet equally applicable to Sulla or Barroso.

After the siege of Athens, expect a march upon the capital....The verdict is out on whether it be in the name of self-ordained Caesars of a European Empire, or in the name of national state democracy.

Yours,

(for freedom and democracy)

Steven Parris Ward.

Reasons to be concerned about Barroso's State of the Union speeches (2011-2012).

To the free minded Libertarians of Europe,

Here are some of Mr. Barroso's worrying utterances that reveal his fundamentalist views are more radical than might be supposed:

1. *"globalization demands more European unity. More unity demands more integration. More integration demands more democracy, European democracy."*

A cabal of Commissars, none of whom can be sacked, and who aren't properly elected by the peoples of Europe, cannot be said to be a true democracy, but only a federal tyranny, or an oligarchy. To "demand" makes no acknowledgement of concession to the will of the people, nor Parliamentary debate.

2. *"when you are on a boat in the middle of the storm, absolute loyalty is the minimum you demand from your fellow crew members."*

The Euro Titanic is sinking. Many people want to revert to national currencies and devalue. Many want referenda to demonstrate we still live in politically accountable democracies. The Captain is screaming and demanding for his crew members and passengers to stay on board. He is offering veiled threats if they do not follow his orders. Meanwhile, some crew members are sensibly urging the Captain that the passengers need to abandon ship. They need to be helped into independent lifeboats because the ship is going down.

3. *"a federation"* is now required *"to win the battle against nationalists, or extreme populists."*

In Barroso's world, "nationalists and populists" must be expunged from the European Union. Flag waving may be an act of national populism and patriotism, beloved by the majority, but it will not be tolerated above the European identity. The EU Federal State trumps over a person's country, its unique culture and democracy.

4. *"It was an illusion to think that we could have a common currency and a single market with national approaches to economic and budgetary policy. Let's avoid another illusion that we can have a common currency and a single market with an*

intergovernmental approach. For the euro area to be credible – and this is not only the message of the federalists, we need a truly Community approach."

For Barroso, national democracies must be subjugated to the Community method. For Community substitute Communist, which is what this undemocratically "elected" Commission President, a former Maoist Communist, has striven for all his political life. Such goals and aims will continue to be effected by the strategies of the Cultural Marxists at the community/ county council and grassroots level, as national democracies are dismantled and national cultures and economies are absorbed and ruled. No intergovernmental discussion, effectively indicates the impotence of national democracies within the EU autocratic set up.

5. *"it may be necessary to consider further changes to the Treaty. I am also thinking particularly of the constraint of unanimity. The pace of our joint endeavour cannot be dictated by the slowest."*

No unanimity equals qualified majority voting. Yet QMV equals a tyranny if the unelected cabal determines policy via the unelected Commission over the Parliament. In this, the Commission determines the right to press ahead with what is in the best interests of ensuring state power and totalitarian control, irrespective of individual member states wishes to the contrary.

6. *"We gain a European identity and citizenship apart from our national citizenship. European citizenship adds a set of rights and opportunities. The opportunity to freely cross borders, to study and work abroad. Here again, we must all stand up and preserve and develop these rights and opportunities. Just as the Commission is doing now with our proposals on Schengen. We will not tolerate a rolling back of our citizens' rights. We will defend the freedom of circulation."*

Flooding countries with countless immigrants, until a country's infrastructure is no longer capable of supporting said numbers, is an effective means of usurping and weakening national economies- justifying centralised control. Multiculturalism weakens national cultural identity. A weak national economy, national culture, and national democracy, subjugated to a European Collective Federal Government, enslaves and does not free people. It only further strengthens a European model of undemocratic one State rule. This is a question of space not race. Multiculturalism has failed. It has sown the seeds of civil and ethnic discontent through encouraging cultural disparity, ghettos, and a sense of alienation. It has undermined national cultural identity, which should above all be readily identifiable and unified.The spectrum of differing cultural identies forged over centuries cannot be easily merged through the insistence and imposition of a totalitarian political construct. The cultural problems and civil disobedience exhibited by the former Soviet Union, and indeed its subsequent collapse, provide a historical testament to this fact.

Barroso finds nationalism and the populist view a danger to further EU control. He doesn't want to "engage in semantic discussions," like a true democrat would. He stresses instead the need to take a federal path exhibiting "solidarity", which he believes is "the only realistic way to achieve progress in Europe." In this he advocates a desire to "win the battle against nationalists, or extreme populists". A bigoted, judgemental view point.

At least comrade Barroso recognises that national democracies, and the rights of the individual over the tyranny of collectivism, and the corrupt, undemocratic Federal State of the EU, is popular. People have died to preserve such individual freedoms in the name of national democracies, liberty and freedom in two World Wars. To the people of Europe, I urge them to continue to fight for democracy and liberty if the challenge is laid down. In spite of his veiled threats against the popular view of the majority, that seeks to champion national state democracy, his endeavours to champion the undemocratic oligarchy of EU rule must be resisted. Specifically, I urge all British citizens to protect our Parliamentary Democracy through active voting, our Bill of Rights, Magna Carta and other rules of law which constitute our ancient laws must be championed: views that men are born free, and guided by the law, not that kings rule men, or that absolute state control via politicians should usurp the rights of the individual, or the majority wish. Men are innocent until proven guilty, not guilty until proven innocent. Habeas corpus trumps corpus juris. Politicians are supposed to be our democratically elected representatives not our rulers. Politicians are there to serve us, the people, and our country, not the other way round.

Yours,

(for freedom and democracy)

Steven Parris Ward.

Response to John Major, Daily Telegraph, September 14th on the Move towards a new EU Federation and our position towards it.

"As integration deepens, we will not be alone in seeking a credible structure outside the federal core, but within the single market and the wider EU. A treaty – requiring unanimity – may be necessary"

Dear Mr. Major,

You are wrong again. It seems you didn't pay attention to the State of the Union speech that the undemocratically "appointed" President Barroso (the former Maoist Communist) gave in Brussels recently. I quote:

"it may be necessary to consider further changes to the Treaty. I am also thinking particularly of the constraint of unanimity. The pace of our joint endeavor cannot be dictated by the slowest."

In other words, there will be no unanimity tolerated in forming the new Federation and its treaties. Dissenters who do not display "solidarity" will not be tolerated. "Solidarity" and not "subsidiarity" is the buzz word of the largely Marxist sympathisers that espouse this collectivist EU agenda when they speak their socialist speak.

One wonders, therefore, how a non-Federation country with some aspiration to maintain traces of National State democracy will be treated in a "looser" EU relationship that you and Mr. Cameron suggest, or indeed insist upon, for the wording of any future referendum?

The answer is clear: Britain will be ruled, but not have a seat at the top table for decision making in the new Federation. That is unless they invoke article 50 of Lisbon. Failure to leave means the Federation and its undemocratically "appointed" Commission and President will continue to call the shots. This is irrespective of our stance if we take your leader's options: "IN the Federation or IN but not part of the Federation" strategy. This is is an impotent strategy at best.

EU governance is largely incompatible with the survival of National State democracy Mr. Major. How are we to make decisions if we do not agree with the majority of our EU Commission rulers? Intergovernmental decision making and unanimity decision making will be jettisoned as Barroso makes clear:

"It was an illusion to think that we could have a common currency and a single market with national approaches to economic and budgetary policy. Let's avoid another illusion that we can have a common currency and a single market with an intergovernmental approach. For the euro area to be credible – and this is not only the message of the federalists, we need a truly Community approach."

For "Community approach" substitute decision making akin to a Communist dictatorship; a Politburo ordering a Supreme Soviet what they must rubber stamp. Indeed, any position wishing to maintain national democracy will be seen as an anathema to the Commission's, and by proxy the Federation's aims. In this we will continue to be no more than the dissenters. Here the dissenters in Barroso's own words (Europe Day speech) are :

"...the nationalists and the populists" who "will not be tolerated"

In this, National State democracies will be accepted in Parliament (at least for now), but these must be trumped by European Federal mandates and decision making of the undemocratically elected Commission.

42

Campaigners for National state democracies in Barroso's own words are those that:

"wave the flags of xenophobia" and they *"will not be tolerated".*

Apparently the patriotic flag waving of the national flag has become an act of xenophobia. Was it so at the Olympics?

The Conservative EU paradox of preserving nation state democracy against the Euro regime, versus the advantages of the single market, continues to tear your party apart.

We have two choices in Cameron's plan for a wording of a referendum, none of which are sustainable for national state democracy and independent fiscal decision making.

1. Either we move to deeper integration and join the EZ or New Federal State. Here we have only the pretence of democracy: ruled as we are by the President and unelected Commission over a Parliament that merely rubber-stamps their diktats, but we can at least have possible representation in the Commission. But representation in the Commission necessitates a concern for supranational and not national interests in any case effectively negating national power.

2. We are in a looser arrangement. Here we have no means to suggest laws that might favour our representation in the Commission, but as EU members we do in Parliament. In this, however, we are duty bound to follow the diktats of the Commission, which determines legislation, and thus by virtue of being in the second tier, which does not determine legislation, we are effectively impotent.

Concerning both options, qualified majority voting trumps any "romantic" notions you have of a "unanimity" of consensus. Here, then, we are no more than a vassal satellite state, irrespective of which class we join.

There can be no full repatriation of powers as you full well know in virtue of Lisbon Treaty legislation and the acquis communitaire. Neither will a looser arrangement be possible in present treaties as outlined by 2014/2015 in any case. There is, therefore, only one option: a third clause on the referendum; an out clause, where a trading arrangement, perhaps an EFTA type alliance with the EU is possible, which accepts we are no longer subject to full EU economic and political control.

http://www.youtube.com/watch?v=KMZbs6zu5PU

Yours,

(for freedom and democracy)

Steven Parris Ward.

"Germans are finally losing patience with the euro racket", 19th September 2012.

Dear Mr Hannan,

Your arguments simply expressed are:

1. Black Wednesday wasn't black it was white, because Major and Lamont left the ERM.
Yet the truth is they forced us in without a mandate and remained in against all advice until they were effectively forced out against their wishes. These pro EU federalist pushers nearly destroyed the country's economy, and now these liars are trying to claim a victory. Typical historical revisionist nonsense.

2. The EU will not collapse until the Germans become tired of it.

A very odd and distorted view of German supremacy over the power of Mao Tse Barroso, the unelected Commission, and the Frankfurt Group; all of whom are more than capable of stitching up Germany too with QMV and pre-existing Lisbon legislation in the near future. Since when did a national state democracy rule over the Commission? Evidence of German capitulation to the new Collective Tyranny has already been increasingly clear in Mr Draghi's proposals for increasing ECB centralised powers, unlimited bond buying, and increased periods for loan repayments against the powers of the German Federal Court. Expect their No-Yes answer to yield more acquiescence in the future.

Your real problem here is the tendency to still see the EU in terms of nation state democracies working together, and if the big player leaves it will be over. You haven't yet realised a new supranational political and economic body is being formed that will effectively absorb, rule and finally destroy national state democracies and indeed nationhood. It will be effectively a rule by the European Commission with no full democratic mandate. Neither, if one accepts your correlation, have you fully considered the economic effect on the European Union if you achieve your proclaimed wish, and Britain leaves the EU. A certainly devastating impact as one of its chief contributors. A scenario the EC will do everything to avoid, irrespective of the popular vote, until they have achieved their tyrannical objectives to rule.

3. Concerning dear old Blighty, you still occupy a "false opposition", pro Federal mindset, by virtue of manipulating your position on Europe. You have shifted now to the Cameron view that "we must remain in and claw back power, but not be part of the Federation". Yet this is just a con trick to further capitulation.

For Mr Cameron and the pro EU lobby, I expect his future promise of a referendum on whether to remain in is a mere delaying tactic till Lisbon laws are fully implemented in 2015. Then intergovernmental decision making and veto powers will be effectively abolished. In the meantime the Commission will continue to press for the UK to pay the greatest share of budget responsibility to an organisation lacking the integrity for proper auditing. An effective means to pressure further compliance through economic capitulation.

How can you call yourself a Euro-sceptic, as your leader has the temerity to do also, and lie to the people? There will be no repatriation of powers of any meaningful kind until article 50 is invoked, and you well know it. Yet you support the Cameron position to stay in, and by virtue of it support that an in/out referendum is unnecessary.

The old repatriation of powers fudge is becoming a very poor ploy. Particularly when it is muttered that there will be a possibility of opting back in later. You write articles, but do nothing meaningful in terms of uniting with the true opposition of UKIP. Indeed, you actively seek to split the UKIP vote. and support EU expansion with your association with The Friends of Turkey Campaign also.

Yours,

(for freedom and democracy)

Steven Parris Ward.

Postscript:

I urge all good libertarians in Europe not to underestimate the power of the EU. The media has consistently drummed the message to the people that the EU will imminently collapse. That the Euro will collapse, and that achieving an Out choice on the referendum is largely not the issue; as none of this federalist nonsense is going to last the course in any case. Mr Hannan too has continuously aired the message that the EU and the Euro will imminently collapse. He has spoken of it for years. Farage to his credit has said that until recently he also believed this was the case, but he now realises, and correctly so, the fanaticism of Barroso, Draghi, et al to keep this going whatever the cost to freedom, democracy or national economics. This is indeed "extremely worrying".

These people are fanatics. They seek to trump nation state democracies and decision making. They ignore the demands of the people for a voice. They are prepared to bring country's to their knees to achieve their aims. We actually, at present, only have one way out and that is article 50 of Lisbon. Let us pray this will not become void in future treaties and the exit door to leave, thereby preserving national state democracy and freedom, is not finally locked shut.

" a federation of nation states" is now required "to win the battle against nationalists, or extreme populists."

"It was an illusion to think that we could have a common currency and a single market with national approaches to economic and budgetary policy. Let's avoid another illusion that we can have a common currency and a single market with an intergovernmental approach. " Barroso, State of The Union Speech 2012.

"Sometimes I like to compare the EU as a creation to the organisation of empire. We have the dimension of empire." — José Manuel Barroso, President of the European Commission, EU observer, 10 July 2007

"Our constitution cannot be reduced to a mere treaty for co-operation between governments. Anyone who has not yet grasped this fact deserves to wear the dunce's cap. " — Valéry Giscard, President of the EU Convention, speech in Aachen accepting the Charlemagne Prize (a former Nazi Prize) for European integration, 29th May 2003

The only EU referendum worth holding is one on membership, Daily Telegraph, (21 September 2012).

Dear Mr. Hannan,

Renegotiation before an In/Out referendum is simply a delaying tactic and a deceit. A promise of something that requires unanimity of consensus, and which by 2014 with veto abolition and QMV, cannot happen in any case. Judicial powers can be restored, at least in part. But we need to invoke article 50 before any full repatriation of powers can take place. You have read the Lisbon Treaty and acquis communitaire, and you know the situation. The call for the dismantling of intergovernmental negotiations by Barroso further makes your shopping list null and void. There can be no true and convincing repatriation of powers before article 50 of Lisbon can be invoked.

Your new deceits in support of Cameron mark a shift in position. They appear to be:
1. Manipulate the electorate to remain in the EU with the promise of repatriation. A full repatriation that can't legally happen.

2. Stem the leaking of votes in your inept and mismanaged party, by floating the idea to the BBC that a UKIP/Conservative pact will occur. You know full well this will never happen under a Prime Minister that has labelled them "fruitcakes", "loonies", and "closet racists". Why then do you place your trust in a man who blatantly doesn't seek to leave the EU?

Surely you must realise any idea of a pact will alienate potential centre left voters to UKIP, who cannot trust the Conservatives, their corruption and deceit. If you do realise this I have then identified your very purpose: to split the UKIP vote. Whilst any Faustian pact that might occur (ill-advised in my view) will effectively nullify the possibility of any future in/out referendum.

Are we really supposed to believe that "U turn Cameron" will be true to his word when he has proven himself to be an out and out liar? More pertinently, that he has said we will "never" be allowed the chance to leave the EU on his watch? Mr Miliband and Harriet Harmann have also categorically denied any possibility of a referendum.

The questions remain:
Why do you support a Cameron plebiscite that in effect gives no true in/out choice? You claim you don't, and any such plebiscite would be a gross deception of the British people. Yet you support Mr. Cameron, who is floating such an idea, along with his cohorts such as Liam Fox. You even have the audacity to write a list we could achieve before an in/out referendum would occur. You do this knowing full well such a referendum will not be agreed to.

You do this as a gross deception of the British electorate, when you know full well under Lisbon laws and the strictures of the acquis communitarie that there is only one choice for true repatriation- out. You also do this distorting the fact you are sowing the seeds for a fixed plebiscite, whilst criticising the notion of one. You justify this with the notion of a future in/out referendum post-election. A future referendum, based on past promises, Cameron has no intention of honouring. A further strategy to counter attack the article written by Mr Farage recently, about the history of the Conservatives using fixed plebiscite ploys in the past.

There can be no doubt which side of the fence you now sit on. You campaign for further EU expansion with The Friends of Turkey Campaign, whilst pushing the view that remaining in the EU we can negotiate a fair repatriation of powers. An absurd and downright wicked lie of a position.

Your credentials aren't one of a genuine Euro-sceptic, but more a Cameronite Euro-sceptic: an oxymoron. A con-tradiction in terms.

To sum up, you too are party to a gross deceit. You further your deceit by continually writing as if you speak as an Englishman when you were in fact born and raised in Peru.

I remain sir,

Yours,

(for freedom and democracy)

Steven Parris Ward.

The Queen: why couldn't we arrest Abu Hamza? James Delingpole, Telegraph (25th September 2012).

Mr Delingpole asks: "What has happened to Britain?"

Answer: Cultural Marxism. Implemented under the rubric of political correctness. The creation of trauma through injustice, and an undermined legal and judicial system, with bias against the victims of crime. Two CM proposals which have been progressively implemented, and which are well under way to undermine our country's claim to an independent judiciary. It is designed to make possible the coming Federal State and a centralised and uniform judicial and legal system run from the continent. All perpetrated and made possible through excessive ECHR, ECJ and EU legislation. The claim will be it will be more effective than our present antiquated system.

Britain isn't just at war with Muslim terrorists, it is being thwarted by the ECHR, ECJ and the EU, who are working in tandem to destroy this country's autonomy, its political, military and economic powers, as well as the Monarchy itself. It represent the death of individual freedom and rights.

 http://www.youtube.com/watch?v=sPd0Sg42Cvo

Yours,

(for freedom and democracy),

Steven Parris Ward.

The Lib Dem conference: spare us the job applications for posts in a Labour government, Telegraph, Lord Tebbit, (26th September, 2012).

Dear Lord Tebbitt,

As the Conservative strategy today, judging by some articles in the papers, appears to be to equate Clegg's conference speech with a brand of Toryism, it is refreshing to read your principled evaluation of Clegg's Socialist ideology. An ideology you fruitfully compare with historical comparisons to former Labour Prime Minister Wilson.

I take it one could then express it with the formula:
LibDem + Con= Lab
LibDem+ Lab + Con= EU
Therefore:

EU + EC+ QMV = FU. FU-UK = FSE

A formula that Lord Tebbit should rightly criticise as being opposed to true Conservative values, with its big state, collectivist agenda.

Based on this formula, however it appears the only conclusion is that it leads to an unwanted capitulation to Brussels and rule by an emerging totalitarian Commission: a slow motion coup d'etat. This, it appears, is an aim that Miliband and Clegg, with their Socialist ideals, either welcome whole heartedly, or have not the foresight to see the dangers of, with their desire to remain within an EU set up.

Unfortunately, however we must add Cameron to the formula. The reason being that Cameron, with his left wing Progressive policies, is not a true Tory, but a Liberal.

Little wonder then that Cameron appears to be preparing no more than a fixed plebiscite to remain within the EU set up. Little wonder then he does not react to the European President's speech, that called for an abolition of intergovernmental powers and the administering of QMV. Little wonder he is more concerned with presently running away to the US and advertising the importance of giving away billions to line the pockets of overseas aid barons. Many of whom are demonstrably corrupt. Recent contribution of millions to South Africa have revealed much of the overseas aid went to building a Prime Ministerial mansion filled with expensive cars, and this is but one example.

Mr Cameron is no Conservative. If he were a true Conservative he would be advocating fiscal conservatism. He would also be concerned about Mr. Barroso's speeches, which thematically state that unanimity, and intergovernmental decision making should no longer be deemed necessary. He would be addressing the people in preparation for a referendum.

The PM does not appear to realise that British democracy and meaningful decision making will be but a historic relic if we remain part of the EU. We will not be in the Federation, neither will we have any meaningful power in the second tier. Why does he not seek to offer a full in/out referendum? Why does he insist the British people will never be permitted the right to invoke article 50 whilst he is PM?

In short, why is the PM refusing the British people, who he supposedly represents, the right to express their view with a clear democratic mandate? Why is he preparing to offer a fudge on a referendum, whilst still claiming he is going to be "at the top table" in Europe? Neither he, nor Mr Clegg, nor indeed Mr Miliband, with his recent denial of the possibility of a referendum, have the right to deny the people that they represent the freedom of choice.

Yours,

(for freedom and democracy)

Steven Parris Ward.

David Cameron braves David Letterman's US chat show – and leaves red-faced; Telegraph (27th September 2012).

Dear Mr Letterman,

During your prime time tv show Prime Minister Cameron said:

"I think it's very important we keep our own currency... I think in Europe, if you've got a single currency, you are going to end up effectively with some form of single government. I don't want that for Britain. We are part of Europe, we trade, we co-operate, we work together. But I don't want to be part of a country called Europe. I want to be part of a country called Great Britain."

So Mr. Cameron doesn't want to be ruled by the European Union? Yet he wants to remain in the European Union? He says he doesn't want a single government? What he wants then are two governments? But this is effectively what we have at the moment David: the British government and the EU government. Unfortunately the EU government tells Britain what to do.

One presumably would want to make a distinction between being a lover of Europe and being a member of the European Union. Unfortunately for Mr Cameron, however, a specific statement was given in relation to Britain's relationship with Europe recently, when he categorically stated Britain will not be given the opportunity to leave the EU, at least whilst he remains the Prime Minister.

Doesn't Mr. Cameron realise if we remain part of the European Union marriage, that the EU government will effectively rule us and the British government will be completely impotent under a federal autocracy and QMV? Doesn't he realise intergovernmental agreements are being abolished? Doesn't he realise not being part of the new Federation government, whilst remaining on the periphery, will effectively mean we are even weaker, with no voice at all? Yet we will still have to abide by its rulings if we remain in the emerging USE?

He appears to be confused, not only about the Magna Carta, but about the Lisbon Treaty and its articles.

Until he invokes article 50 of Lisbon, via an in/out referendum, there can be nothing other than a system where an EU government increasingly rules us and determines what we want to do. A two government system is no system at all. There can only be British home rule for Britain. One government, but it must be British. We can then negotiate trade agreement from a position of strength with the EU. Doesn't this guy get it?

As an Englishman I felt embarrassed and ashamed Mr. Cameron couldn't translate basic Latin after attending Eton and Oxford. Also, that he clearly didn't know some of the basic principles of the Magna Carta- one of the documents used as reference in the founding of the US constitution. It explains why he appears not to appreciate the importance of habeas corpus. It explains why he has sacrificed it to Lisbon rulings of corpus juris; enabling British Citizens to be imprisoned overseas, and arrested without evidence needing to be presented first before a court. It explains why he ignores the rights of the people to an in/out referendum.

Mr. Johnson has leapt to Mr. Cameron's defence with the claim that it was a deliberate ploy designed to show Mr. Cameron's "demotic credentials". He did not wish to appear overly intelligent having "Latin pouring from every orifice" and thus feigned ignorance. An assumption sadly which serves only to emphasise what contempt (if true) the Prime Minister holds the general British people in; as it presumes a standard of ignorance in respect to the meaning of the basic words Magna Carta- words any school boy or girl might be expected to know. Such a ploy, at the present time, is a presumption hardly advisable considering the current Plebgate scandal of Andrew Mitchell. As for the more difficult content it might be summarised with these words of advice:

Mr. Cameron, you have no "divine right of a king" to override our laws or ignore our wishes. You are our elected representative and you must follow the people's law!

Yours,

(for freedom and democracy)

Steven Parris Ward.

"I'm sorry to say it , but my old school chum isn't PM material. The party leader and I go back a long way, but the time has come for a few political truths", Boris Johnson, Telegraph (1st October 2012)

Dear Mr. Johnson,

You profess to tell us the truth about your former school chum. Why not tell us of the more important truths? Why not tell us of the other school you attended: The European School of Brussels? Why not tell us you were born in New York of former European Commission employee parentage? This background information then helps to explain why you, a self- professed "Euro-sceptic", are in reality nothing of the kind. It helps to explain why you support The Friends of Turkey Campaign for EU expansion. It helps explain why you do not advertise London jobs properly in Britain, but advertise them in East European job centres. It helps explain your pro Schengen, multicultural, "let's have an open border policy" bias.

Do you sleep at night knowing you are promoting an undemocratic increasingly tyrannical organisation in Brussels? An organisation that is turning into a Soviet style oligarchy? Do you sleep knowing you support the EU, whose stated aims will destroy British autonomy and sovereignty? If you were a British patriot you wouldn't. You Sir, are no Conservative, and neither are you a British patriot. Your knowledge of our British sporting achievements is lousy too.

No- Marxist Miliband isn't PM material, but neither is your pro EU leader Mr Cameron. Neither for that matter are you.

Yours,

(for freedom and democracy)

Steven Parris Ward.

"We are luckier than we realise to have had Labour as our Left-of-Centre party", reply to Dan Hannan, 2nd Oct 2012, Daily Telegraph.

Dear Mr. Hannan,

The seemingly benign Labour Party appears so only due to its adoption of Fabian principles: an imposition of neo-Marxist principles by stealth. The ideology and its aims are no less dangerous than the avowed principles of the overt Anarchists, the Cultural Marxists, or indeed the Communist Party itself.

Lest we forget, the Fabian Society hosted as one of its most notable speakers Lenin himself. Bernard Shaw (a cheerleader of eugenics and mass murder by gas) called him "the greatest of Fabians". He went further:

"the Russian communism is nothing more than the putting into practice of the Fabian programme which we have been preaching the last forty years".

Whilst the Fabians denied the necessity for the proletarian class struggle, as well as the socialist revolution along military or violent lines, they contended that the transition from capitalism to socialism could be effected through gradual, incremental change. In this, the Lenin / Sun Tzu strategy- a strategy also employed by the Russian Soviets and the East Germans- was adapted. It sought to use the military strategy of "adopting the mask of the enemy", whilst gradually wearing down their opponents through the strategy of Fabius (the Roman tactician) through a stealth war of attrition. In this, they also sought to "appear weak" as part of their Communist infiltration. Through their covert strategy, they have found happy comradeship with the Cultural Marxists ever since.

Lenin himself defined Fabianism as an extremely opportunist trend that employed the advantages of "the useful idiot" to the great cause. Blair, a President of that society, with his benign appearance, has more than justified the strengthening of the One State Socialist cause. The dismantling of our sovereignty, and the absorption of Britain into the new emerging Federal State, is well on course. Its undemocratic nature is apparently a deficit not worth addressing as a matter of urgency by any of the three main parties. Evidence to date in policy and centre left ideology indicates they have all been successfully infiltrated.

Hobsbawm was not alone in his dismissal of the horrors of history which the Fabians and their political arm- the Labour Party- have sought to impose on the people of this country. Shaw's public defence of Stalin's Great Terror is a good example of many who when pressed justified the cause:

"Even in the opinion of the bitterest enemies of the Soviet Union and of her government, the [purge] trials have clearly demonstrated the existence of active

conspiracies against the regime… I am convinced that this is the truth, and I am convinced that it will carry the ring of truth even in Western Europe, even for hostile readers."

Shaw likewise defended Stalin's mass executions, scolding:

"we cannot afford to give ourselves moral airs when our most enterprising neighbour… humanely and judiciously liquidates a handful of exploiters and speculators…"

In 1949 he even wrote a defence of Stalin's pseudo-scientific Lysenkoism. D.H. Lawrence also shamefully supported such measures.

A Labour "useful idiot" working for peace, social reforms and economic egalitarianism to destroy the class system is all very well and good- as both Stalin and Lenin realised. Let us not forget, however, the long road to where it has in the past led. Often idealists can be fruitfully used for misguided aims. The road to hell is paved with good intentions. History condemns the collectivist ethos. The death of millions, and the destruction of living cultures, has been the evidence of its implementation.

Even today many have been misguided and joined its ranks, lulled by the security, wealth and comfort which democracy and free enterprise capitalism affords. The extent to which collectivism has destroyed democracy and constitutional rule, morals and community values, particularly in the Republic of the USA, is little understood and grossly underestimated. The chaos of the Cultural Marxist principles both in America and in this country to effect Socialist aims for statist rule in Europe, or indeed an eventual One World Government, have brought in the last 50 years only cultural decay, government expansion, bureaucratic chaos and less personal freedom. We need more individualism and less government intervention and expenditure for a better world.

http://www.youtube.com/watch?v=zPOIOUq2eBY

Yours,

(for freedom and democracy)

Steven Parris Ward.

"David Cameron's referendum dilemma", Daniel Hannan, Telegraph (9th October 2012)

"...a couple of weeks ago, there was a change of heart. The PM still planned to make his announcement, we were told, but it would come later in the year. The reason was that he was engaged in a separate argument with Brussels to do with the budget – specifically, we now learn, his laudable attempt to create separate budgets for eurozone and non-eurozone states – and he felt that a referendum announcement in the middle of those talks would weaken his position."

Dear Mr Hannan,

Mr Cameron used the same kind of excuse for not announcing a specific date for a referendum in his pre- election pledge. Then, he claimed, he was unable to announce a referendum until the ratifications of member state countries have been completed, as it would compromise their decision making.

https://www.youtube.com/watch?v=Dz6k173Yn1g

There is a further suggestion that even if the treaty is ratified, he will not announce a referendum in any case. This has now been proven to be his position as he is denying Britain the referendum post Lisbon. What utter rhetorical balderdash!

David Cameron only has one choice: he must give a definite date for an in/out referendum, and he must announce that date before the next general election. It is his only chance of regaining the electorate's trust. If he can make the case that his present negotiations have delayed an immediate announcement, he yet might regain support.

Any other attempt to repatriate powers piecemeal is a lost cause. Wolfgang Schäuble and the Commission have made it clear that they are in no mood to repatriate powers during the present crisis. It is clear also any demand for repatriation of powers would severely harm the ability to negotiate particular specifics in future negotiations- should we remain in without invoking article 50 of Lisbon. This is based on the ill will that earlier repatriation attempts would provoke.

Further problems arise in 2014/2015, as intergovernmental negotiations are being dismantled. The unanimity problem is therefore a non-starter, as full QMV is being introduced. This, however, is no guarantee of swifter repatriation.

In any case, there is a view that the EU's acquis communautaire is sacrosanct. It cannot therefore be amended without leaving. Appreciable powers for considerable repatriation have therefore been curtailed.

The EU Glossary compiled by the European Commission defines the acquis as follows:

"The acquis communautaire or Community patrimony is the body of common rights and obligations which bind all the Member States together within the European Union. It is founded principally on the Treaty of Rome and the instruments that

supplement it (the Single European Act, the Treaty on European Union etc.), plus the wide range of secondary legislation enacted under them. The acquis communautaire relates mainly to the single market and the four freedoms inherent in it: freedom of movement for goods, persons, capital and services, the common policies which underpin it (agriculture, trade, competition, transport and others) and measures to support the least favoured regions and categories of the population. The Union has committed itself to maintaining the acquis communautaire in its entirety and developing it further. Exemptions and derogations from the legal framework constituted by the acquis communautaire are granted only in exceptional circumstances and are limited in scope. "

Article B of the Treaty on European Union (the Maastricht Treaty) is believed to have given force to the concept, as it stated that one of the objectives of the Union was:

"to maintain in full the acquis communautaire and build on it ... "

Further, existing Member States are obliged to respect the acquis as a dynamic concept which is constantly evolving. Treaty amendment has formed (and will continue to form) the evolution of the EU. It ought to follow that a Treaty amendment to remove a competence from the EU is as much an evolutionary development of the acquis as adding a competence – it is just that the former has not happened in practise, and with such Euro fanaticism appears unlikely. Will Cameron be the first? It seems unlikely.

Court of Justice judges interpret EU law in the light of Treaty amendment in their rulings, and so the process of change and evolution continues, even though Court of Justice decisions cannot be amended. In any case, many believe that the doctrine of the "occupied field" prevents the repatriation of powers in areas in which the EU has law-making competence. When this happens, Member States lose their competence in this area, even if the EU has not yet legislated. Thus, if the EU is given the power under the Treaties to take legislative action in a particular area, this inhibits Member States from acting. This is in case their laws are subsequently found to be incompatible with EU law (pre-emption). The EU's power to act in that area is therefore guaranteed forever.

The point of all this is clear: even if Mr Cameron sincerely wanted to repatriate whilst remaining in the EU he hasn't a snowball in Hell's chance of succeeding. Based on his continuous shifting and avoidance tactics also, it appears unlikely he will be able to convince either his party, or the electorate, that he is genuinely concerned about the imminent loss of British sovereignty, or British political and economic powers.

Yours,

(for freedom and democracy)

Steven Parris Ward.

"Unprising the EU's Iron Grip." Telegraph 16th October 2012.

To the Free minded Peoples of Europe,

A great deal of the media coverage that recently focused on the awarding of the Peace Prize to the EU omitted to mention that Thorbjen Jagland is currently not only the chairman of the Norwegian Nobel Committee, but also secretary-general of the Council of Europe. This Council acts as the primary propaganda agent for further integration and unification of the EU. The Council of Europe, the EU and its predecessors, have been closely associated since the 1950s. Impartiality in prize giving is therefore revealed as bias.

During the 1970's, Jagland, a former Norwegian prime minister, was a one time agent/informant of the Soviet KGB (code name "Jurij"). Jagland's political pedigree supports this leaked information. He was a member of the Workers' Youth League: a Norwegian communist organization, that was formed with the merger in 1927 of the Left Communist Youth League and the Socialist Youth League of Norway. Jagland eventually became national president of the Workers' Youth League from 1977 to 1981. Norway's current prime minister, Jens Stoltenberg, was also a former national president of the Worker's Youth League, and has also been identified as a former KGB asset (codenamed "Steklov.").

Jagland is also a leader of Norway's Labour Party, which is officially a member party of the Socialist International: the global coalition of socialist and communist parties. One of its announced objectives is the end of national sovereignty, and the creation of a world government.

On September 12, 2012, Mr Barosso remained true to this cause when he called for a sweeping away of the last vestiges of national sovereignty, and the transformation of the EU into a unified federation; a goal the architects have been pursuing from the beginning, but denying to the public until relatively recently.

Barroso, a former prime minister of Portugal, was a former member of the Portuguese Workers' Communist Party, a violent, revolutionary organization that advocated the violent revolutionary ideology of Communist China's Chairman Mao. His activities since his supposed conversion to moderation indicate that he didn't leave his radicalism behind. His use of the term "populism" was an obsession he has articulated both in his early pro Maoist speeches. and in his recent speeches in the European Parliament.

http://www.youtube.com/watch?v=wCt7PPVXzzE

As Jesus once said "by your fruits shall ye be known". Thus, his team unsurprisingly consist of the following:

Mr Barrot, who took on Transport. In 2000 he received an eight-month suspended jail sentence for his involvement in an embezzlement case and was banned from holding public office for two years.

Mr Kovács, who took on Taxation. For many years he was a Communist apparatchik, a friend of Mr Kádár, the dictator in Hungary, and an outspoken opponent of the values that we cherish in the West. His new empire will focus on taxation policy, and he will oversee the customs union from Cork to Vilnius.

Finally, a Mr Kallas, who for 20 years was a Soviet Party apparatchik. That is until his newly acquired taste for capitalism got him into trouble: he was acquitted of abuse and fraud, but convicted for providing false information. He is now unsurprisingly in charge of the EU's anti-fraud drive.

Yours,

(for freedom and democracy)

Steven Parris Ward.

On Daniel Hannan's vague reference to the "Founding Fathers" of the EU- (October 2012).

Dear Mr Hannan,

This was a lucid and entertaining discussion. It focused on the main themes for justifying an in/out referendum with passion and gusto. Thank you for your demonstration. It was also reassuring to hear you speak of your wish for a specific in/out referendum in this video blog in the context of your thoughts about the moral and political deficits of the European Union.

This was something far more akin to the Hannan of old, who appeared indifferent to the diktats of Mr. Cameron's line- that a compromise plebiscite should be offered to the electorate. I amongst many feel glad you are swimming once more in far more UKIP friendly waters. You also appear to have rediscovered your truthful voice, which I feel suits you better than echoing the Party rhetoric of the Conservative leader.

To be frank Mr Cameron's pseudo repatriation of powers line appears disingenuous. A mere ploy to try and appease the electorate, whilst he seeks to ensure an increasingly unlikely second term. The public realise, however, that a repatriation of powers (at least in any real sense) is impossible under the strictures of the acquis communitaire and the treaty of Lisbon. His recent statement, claiming he sought an opt out of EU judiciary powers, which would be later taken back on board- thanks to the former provisos of Tony Blair- appeared an absurd admittance of the fact.

The bottom line, which should inform politicians and the electorate at large, is whether a referendum is" right in principle". It surely must be addressed in that fashion, but too often it is judged in terms of a successful likely outcome; a personal concern to be on the side of the winner. Yet if one forms decisions, as so many MP's do today, only to garner the honours of a more successful political career, justice and truth are forsook, and the integrity of Parliamentary democracy, as a consequence, wrongly becomes of secondary importance.

In this vein, your reference to the "Founding Fathers" of the EU was, in my opinion, rather vague. You mentioned the 1930's, and their dissatisfaction with plebiscitory democracy. This, you claim, led to demagoguery and eventual Fascism and war. Why not speak clearly and directly?

The "Founding Fathers" you are referring to were in fact former Nazis, who outlined initially plans for such a political and economic union in the 1930's. Specifically the Europaische Wirtshaftsgemeinschaft endorsed by Ribbentrop. However, this was not approved until 1943.

Even if the official story is accepted, that this organisation was founded as a "Coal and Steel Community" in the 1950's, all the evidence thus released supports the view that the EU was indeed founded by these " former" Nazis under Adenauer. The list being:

Walter Hallstein: a trained "Nazi Leadership Officer" . He promoted Nazism in German Universities and via the Law. Hallstein became the First President of the European Commission in 1957.

Paul Henri Spaak: who openly rejected democracies in favour of fascist powers. He warned the Allies not to attack Germany through Belgium. He became another "Founding Father" of the European Union. Walter Funk: a Minister under Goebbels at the Nazi Propaganda Ministry, and who was also Reich Economics Minister. He was responsible for dispossessing Jews of their property. He wrote the economic blueprint for a united Europe adopted by the European Union. He was employed in the Lower Saxony Education Ministry from 1957 to 1960, and was an associate of Adenauer.

Hans Josef Globke was responsible for drafting the Nuremburg Race Laws. He became Director of the German Chancellor's Office from 1953 to 1963. This was when the European Economic Community was first officially spoken of and created.

All in fact were active in the Nazi Party when the embryonic European Economic Union was suggested to Hitler as an alternative proposal for a centralised, Nazi led, government of Europe in the 1930's. The difficulty of Adenauer's control of these characters has been well documented.

The idea of a group of Nazi founders who considered democracy an anathema then is not confusing as you state, but makes perfect sense. A loose parallel might be made with the "Founding Fathers" of America, who also had a mistrust for democracy; believing as they did that this form of government only led to chaos. Hence the superior Republican based constitution of the United States. It would be fallacy of course to suppose that due to such comparisons these men were fascist in their political sympathies, or advocated totalitarianism. They were however "anti democratic", at least in the qualified sense, whilst advocating a representative elite selected by democratic process, with sensible checks and balances to curb any totalitarian power that might emerge through the limits of the Constitution.

Concerning the EU, of course the elites former political affiliations are no guarantee of their concerns in the 1950's. These former Nazis may even have been well intentioned. However, one would think that democracy, and the protection and integrity of it as a means of government, would have been foremost in their minds. This, particularly after making the mistakes and suffering the horrors of National Socialism. Unless, of course, their National Socialist sympathies were in fact still live. The dominance of a more technocratically orientated model over the more democratically minded themes of a Republic in the 1950's have led some to suppose this.

Today the bias towards technocracy in the emerging tyranny of the EU is still apparent. It is reinforced by large corporations, and a former Soviet bloc mindset which also appears to consider a democratic deficit is unimportant. Past history shows otherwise. There is little credence to suppose that further federalisation and solidarity towards closer union will address the democratic deficit that now exists. Indeed, it only appears to be worsening. More worrying, however, is the myopia of a PM who appears unable or unwilling to recognise its dangers.

http://www.youtube.com/watch?v=7Nf5KeC4dAs

Yours,

(for freedom and democracy)

Steven Parris Ward.

"EC rule, and the weakening of democratic accountability with separatism in new emerging states" (20th October 2012).

Addressed to those who seek independence whilst remaining in the European Union:

In addition to the move for Catalonia to be separated from Spain, and Scottish independence from the UK, the current popularity of the New Flemish Alliance Party in Belgium suggests Flanders too may lead to separation. All these countries appear to be undergoing some form of separatism, as did Czechoslovakia into Slovakia and the Czech State.

Some might see independence as a move towards autonomy, but it is not if emerging states remain under the control of the European Commission. It actually means little unless article 50 is invoked, facilitating a full break from EU control. It is in fact an EC checkmate in their favour.

The irony that Belgium, whose capital is Brussels, is being effectively split surely cannot be lost on the Commission- when it often displays a desire for increased bureaucracy, with less democratic accountability for nation states, by adhering to a "divide and conqueror" approach.

Whilst separatism supposes increased independence, remaining in provides anything but for both the Flemish, Scots, Catalans, Spanish and indeed the remainder of the UK. Indeed, independence only serves to increase the strength which the EC exerts upon more manageable, separate and weaker states (this being achieved via a lessened majority for QMV, based on size and population). Particular regional needs would most likely find little representation- or unanimity for common concerns- to out vote a large bloc of unified states. Smaller states incidentally, whilst wielding less power, yet provide further Kommissars (as opposed to larger states) increasing the pigs at the trough.

Concerning separatism, Vice-President of the European Commission Viviane Reding has stated that there is no international law that says Catalonia would have to leave the EU if it became independent. This equally applies to Scotland, one presumes, which undermines the Unionist argument that they would have to re-apply for EU membership after the vote for independence in the 2014 referendum.

Commenting, SNP Roderick Campbell – who sits on the European and External Relations Committee – said:

"Viviane Reding's comments in relation to Catalonia are an important confirmation of the fact that there is simply no provision for an independent Scotland to be removed from the EU."

Further: "Scotland is part of the territory of the European Union and the people of Scotland are citizens of the EU – there is no procedure for either of these circumstances to change upon independence, and the rest of the UK will be exactly the same position. We will both be successor states, with exactly the same status within the EU..."

From the EU/EC perspective, the move to separatism would certainly pose less political threat from once powerful nations in any QMV decision making- a process largely ruled by Germany- whilst it would increase the Commissions' power- decreasing a nation states' democratic voice. It is crazy, therefore, to suppose any move to independence should equate to continued EU membership. Sensibly it should signify the end, and yet it does not.

Independence from the EU should be sought, particularly as Barroso has called (in his State of the Union speech) for an end to unanimity of consensus and intergovernmental decision making. Yet incredibly those that speak of "independence" all champion the EU cause of membership, rather than merely a looser free trade arrangement outside of the Euro Zone. This is a popular view in all of the main political parties advocating independence, and a requirement under Lisbon for continued membership in any case.

Examples of adherents of the view are as follows:

- The N-VA. This group support subsidiarity whilst proclaiming, along with other Europe Free Alliance stateless members, integration in Europe. Their mantra is summed up as: "Necessary in Flanders, useful in Europe."
- Another EFA member being the Scottish Nationalists, continued membership fits for Alex Salmond, who strongly desires to associate with the EU and remain within "the family of the EU". He proclaims this whilst stating he is tired of this "UK nonsense"; speaking in words tantamount to suggesting it is a tyranny that robs the Scots of its own voice. A bizarre notion considering devolution and the number of Scots MPs that sit in Westminster. Where incidentally is our English Parliament? Mr Salmond appears either to be inviting acquiescence to the EU, or he is deluded as to the nature of qualified majority voting and the dictatorial whims of the European Commission to manage him.
- Furthermore, spokespeople for the Commission often wish to give the notion that the majority of Catalans favour continued EU membership.
- Also, to date, Cameron has given no indication that a Yes vote to Scottish independence would fundamentally alter the English position on remaining within the EU. It clearly does however, at least in terms of negotiating power. Neither does he appear to be particularly concerned about accepting the 16 year old vote in Scotland; an age group which is clearly aligned to strengthen an independence statistic.

Unfortunately, whilst all appear to be campaigning or moving towards a strengthening of subsidiarity- with a desire to restore, or maintain national powers- all the indicators are an EC oligarchy, and a strengthening and extending of areas of competences for the Commission. These EC competences override subsidiarity at the national level. The main areas to further strengthen their dictatorial rule being:

(a) The internal market
(b) social policy
(c) conomic, social and territorial cohesion
(d) agriculture and fisheries, excluding the conservation of marine biological resources
(e) environment
(f) consumer protection
(g) transport
(h) trans-European networks
(i) energy
(j) area of freedom, security and justice in consultation with ECJ
(k) common safety concerns in public health matters
(l) technological development and space, (those these shall not be limited solely by EC decision making).
(m) Humanitarian aid (though these shall not be limited solely by EC decision making).
Added to these of course will be centralised financial, economic and budget decision making, as well as centralised banking; as determined by EC directives in the new fiscal compact.

Independence without leaving the EU is no independence at all. Repatriation of powers are increasingly less likely in the light of current developments towards centralised control. Furthermore, repatriation of powers now appear to be a costly affair, invoking possible fines, and a begrudging anti nationalistic sentiment by the Commission. Independence as separatism from former states, whilst remaining within the EU, signifies further erosion of democracy and democratic accountability under European Commission jurisdiction. Leaving and rejoining further enforces the necessity of joining the Euro.

http://www.youtube.com/watch?v=K3T1tl4mQKk

http://www.youtube.com/watch?v=o3Od1DaDoV4

http://www.youtube.com/watch?v=cWL1UzPTdaA

Yours,

(for freedom and democracy)

Steven Parris Ward.

"The BBC's inbred culture and politically correct thought have ruined this valuable institution. Time for fresh blood" Lord Tebbit, (24th Oct 2012).

Dear Lord Tebbitt,

So we started with Lord Reith: a proven Nazi sympathiser during World War II, and perhaps the chief reason why Winston Churchill was banned from its airwaves for an extensive period of time preceding the war. We end (hopefully) with an organisation under Chris Patten: another one of those Conservatives who appears to display all the qualities of a "Progressive" left wing propogandist. He who seeks to protect an organisation that peddles a pro EU, politically correct, Cultural Marxist agenda.

Today Lord Patten is reported to be threatening the government if they question the BBC's "impartiality" regarding its ability to conduct an "independent" inquiry into the charge it protected paedophiles. Such veiled threats alone should be sufficient to launch a true "independent" government enquiry of the BBC- if any such thing is possible now for our endemically corrupt institutions- it probably isn't.

The BBC, in this affair, has shown itself to be utterly contemptuous of the truth. It demonstrates its desire to disguise the facts, blame innocents, and protect those responsible. This, plus the fact it is the media mouth for another corrupt organisation that funds it- the EU- fills any decent British citizen with disgust.

It is becoming so increasingly removed from mainstream public opinion now that the license fee is tantamount to a tax without representation. Something it has in common with its partner organisation, the European Union, with its fiscal compact tax.

Its continued existence makes a mockery of our justice system, and any notions that we live in a true democracy. How can it justify its existence as serving the good of the country, when it clearly supports a supranational organisation that strives to destroy British national state democracy and British cultural identity?

http://en.wikipedia.org/wiki/John_Reith,_1st_Baron_Reith

Yours,

(for freedom and democracy)

Steven Parris Ward.

Reply to D. Hannan, Daily Telegraph 12th November 2012, concerning the EU and its non socialist concerns.

"No one claims that the Commission is socialist. The problem is that it is corporatist: an alliance of big businesses, big trade unions and big lobbyists united by their distrust of the electorate"

Dear Mr Hannan,

The European Commission might well be striving to create an inverted totalitarianism, which finds its anonymity in the corporate state.

https://www.youtube.com/watch?v=nelGtSOimwQ

However, whether it be a classical or an inverted form, it is a totalitarian model that it seeks to create, and in this the peoples of Europe are travelling a pathway to serfdom. In this one must not overlook the ideology of the political leaders seeking to create it: M. Barrosso a former Maoist Communist and A. Merkel from the former Eastern bloc, along with a number of former Soviet communists in the Parliament. Such former ideologies are not easily renounced, and mask themselves in various political, supposedly "democratic" guises. I believe many term themselves Social Democrats in the Parliament and Commission.

As for the Long March towards totalitarianism and the communist heaven that these individuals once espoused, but have not apparently formerly renounced, let us not overlook their numerous comrades in such parties as:

http://en.wikipedia.org/wiki/Party_of_European_Socialists

All belong to the Socialist International, whose aim is the dismantling of national state democracies, the implementation of a globalist agenda, and the move towards a one world government, which appears to be unconcerned with democratic principles of rule.

Concerning the Commission, Vaclav Klaus reminds us in his excellent book "Europe: the shattering of Illusions" (p. 70), that it is a body not concerned with the practise of politics, which in its nature causes conflict and dispute, but a cabal that seeks to construct an "anti-politics", in order to pursue peace. It assumes that politics can be "dissipated away by administration". The result is a totalitarian state, on the way to the supposed peaceful utopia of a "non-state", where disputes and conflict are resolved and indeed no more. A view that notes the transitional stage of an unelected one party organising body to effect this.

Bukowski has noted the similarities between the old Soviet system of Politburo and Supreme Soviet and its analogies with the current EU set up. A comparison based on experience:

http://www.youtube.com/watch?v=bM2Ql3wOGcU

The historical progression from totalitarianism to supposedly peaceful Communism is a view outlined by Marx in his "The Poverty of Philosophy", where he states the ultimate aim will be the "withering of the state" as an attack on Capitalism, in order to accomplish the eventual Communist utopia. History to date has shown that this path leads only to the death of democracy, and has so far resulted in a 100 million deaths. The current civil unrest in Greece and the imposition of technocrats in Greece and Italy over elected governments should be viewed as warning signs as to a possible determined future.

Further, your naive claim of political impartiality in the Commission also rather ignores the Marxist leanings of the Socialist ideologues in its midsts, and also the Collectivist ideology of its chief proponents. This ideology remains fundamentally strong. Your view also rather ignores the fact our next Prime Minister might well be Mr Miliband- a self-professed Marxist and Fabian admirer of the neo Left, who will be sympathetic to their aims. Why?

The history of politics should be characterised by the dialectic of critical discussion and debate. Our traditions in this are the basis of Western Civilisation. Democratic methodology is one that is fundamentally Socratic. It should by its nature be impassioned, confrontational, good natured argument. An inverted Hegelian dialectic, that seeks its stasis and culmination in the muzzled silence of a synthesised utopia, for the end game of "peace", has no place in a continually evolving, civilised society. Ultimately, such an end can accommodate neither Conservatives nor Progressives, nor the luxury of freedom of speech presently afforded to both.

http://www.youtube.com/watch?v=ljAANHPkrAE&feature=fvwrel

Yours,

(for freedom and democracy)

Steven Parris Ward.

Benjamin Netanyahu talks of a battle 'between the modern and the medieval.' He is right, and the free world must stand with Israel" Nile Gardiner, Daily Telegraph, November 18th 2012.

Dear Mr Gardiner,

As a general criticism, it might be worth stating that those screaming anti-semitism, against any who profess anything other than a pro-Israel position, appear to understand nothing of the Torah aligned Jews who find Zionism blasphemous and objectionable.

http://www.jewsagainstzionism.com/about/mission.cfm

As many Jews find Zionism objectionable, are we to term these Jews also anti-semitic who oppose the present State of Israel? I think not. One might extrapolate the argument and say that as Muslims too may be defined as being of "semitic" origin, being of the family bloodline of Abraham, this whole anti-Israel equates to anti-semitic argument is pure fallacy.

Bigotry presents itself in many masks and guises, and those crying anti-semitism it appears are those who also feel comfortable labeling all Muslims as terrorists and child rapists when clearly this is not the case. Nothing good may come of bigotry or racism in the current conflict between the Palestinians and the Israelis. Angry bystanders troubled at the violence should not seek to add fuel to the fire.

At the risk of stating the obvious, millions practise both Judaism and Islam who are devout, peace loving, and moral people. Many sects and denominations do not necessarily believe the same thing within the tenets of their own faith. Neither do all Muslims believe in violence (the Sufi view as a notable example), and neither do all Jews believe in the views of Zionism, or even the rights of Jews to live in the current state of Israel. Fundamentalism on both sides can often be used to instil the false values of ignorance, prejudice and hatred- particularly amongst the young.

http://www.youtube.com/watch?v=sVCMGtrsh_8&feature=related

http://www.youtube.com/watch?v=JA6vRC1xW_c

http://www.youtube.com/watch?v=7USXzVwL39g&feature=player_embedded

In relation to my comments I find myself considering Dr Martin Luther King's famous letter in support of the anti-semitic/ anti- zionist relation.

http://en.wikipedia.org/wiki/Letter_to_an_Anti-Zionist_Friend

Such sentiments perhaps would not have been written, if he had himself been more mindful of his more famous utterance, for which he was rightly acclaimed. To whit: "That a man is to be judged not by the colour of his skin, but the content of his character."

I would add to these words my own:

Neither is a man to be judged by his race or his country, but the truth of his words.

Neither is a man to be judged by the tribe birth assigns, but the faith he enacts.

Neither is a man to be judged by the bloodline of family, but his morals and values.

Let each man be judged by his views as a man.

With these distinctions in mind, it is right to cast the conflict within the context of a peace agreement. Further, such an agreement requires an admission of guilt from other parties. Concerning the right for Israel to be a free democracy against the terrible acts of terrorism committed against her people in recent times, and the rights of the Palestinian's to live in peace within recognised boundaries, it is worth stating that there are some who clearly seek to incite Islamic fundamentalism for their own profitable ventures. Such extremism is, in the modern era, being incited to violence by larger forces in the background. The mission of war mongers is still being spread via the Putin funding of Hamas as part of the global Communist agenda. The acts of violence by Israel are still being facilitated by the American right wing fundamentalists and its Corporate fascism, via US military arms sales. Until this is addressed, and the culpability of those named has been properly recognised on both sides, there can only be further escalation and conflicts in the region for political and fiscal purposes. Let us hope that the future is not one of a prophecised Armageddon.

Yours,

(for freedom and democracy)

Steven Parris Ward.

http://en.wikipedia.org/wiki/Russia_and_the_Arab%E2%80%93Israeli_conflict

http://www.jbs.org/news/terrorism-how-russia-is-using-islam-to-build-communism

"We will be popular after we leave the EU", Daniel Hannan, Telegraph: November 21st 2012.

"It's very unusual, in the European Parliament, for people to make a slighting remark about a whole country (as against the leaders of a country who are, obviously, fair game). Except when the country is Britain. It's quite normal for an MEP to preface his remarks with some sneering remark along the lines of: 'The British like to think that they are such gentlemen, but yet again they are being less than honest...' No one would dream of saying such a thing about the Slovenes, the Spanish or the Swedes."

Dear Mr Hannan,

The EU ideologues are beginning to display their true anti-nationalist, anti- democratic colours. They are at last beginning to show they are extreme statists; power hungry Eurocrats, who despise the idea of nation statehood. Theirs is a system of governance that seeks only the freedom to excise the right to be independent, whilst practising the benefits of free enterprise for themselves. More than this, however, the Eurocrats are now sadly revealing themselves as bigots and hate mongers, specifically against the British. A country that with its history has been the example par excellence of what it means to be a great, civilised and free nation. Their venomous utterances reveal only their own prejudices.

It was Milton Friedman and F.A Hayek who warned of the perils upon freedom with economic systems that advocated increased government spending and collectivism. A model the EU is now clearly following. Both academics recognised the slippery road to the totalitarian state that such measures ultimately induced.

Ultimately, the EU can only produce a totalitarian state. Its tendency to enforce this is evident with its empasis on corporate power, and its socialist view of equality of outcome and not equality of opportunity. Individual freedom is circumvented. Alexander Solzhenitsyn is but one writer who has been a witness to such an ideal and its horrible implementation. Its effects upon the individual were chronicled in his descriptions of the gulags of the Soviet Union.

Friedman and Hayek's message is one which appears to have been forgotten by our so called "Conservative" chancellor and Prime Minister. Where is their economic strategy? They display only a schoolboy appreciation of economics with a monetarist quantitative supply solution. This approach coupled with a few feeble, trumped up attempts at clawing back powers from an increasingly menacing, bureaucratic, unaccountable undemocratic power.A power that is corrupt and siphons off the wealth of countries for its own personal and unaccountable ends. Money that is rightfully ours in any case. In such an EU model, with its clear democratic deficit, we are being taxed without proper representation. One cause, lest it be forgotten, that enticed a once former taxed colony of Britain to rightly seek its liberation.

It is unfortunate that it appears Friedman and Hayek's message has also now been forgotten in the USA; as it now follows the empty rhetoric of Obama's increasingly evident, Marxist orientated, wealth distribution for the benefit of the lower class approach. Such an approach- an attempt to reduce all classes to the same denomination in the name of equality- is merely overseeing an inevitable decline. For such wealth distribution involves the hammering of the rich and the stunting of the middle class, who in turn provide and generate the wealth in business and commerce. This can only produce a dead economy, with no growth or jobs in the market, and ultimately an underclass for all. Obama's increasingly centralised, federal government strategies (particularly evident with police and health care policy) signal the death, not only of the true freedom of enterprise, but also democracy, and the constitutionaly orientated and limited government that keeps a culture strong. A massive increase in Federal funded czars appears to be an increasingly EU model of governance.

Mr. Cameron and Mr. Osborne need to take a leaf out of Friedman's "Free to Choose" book. Hayek's warning's too of the dangers of increased centralisation killing the free enterprise market in his "Road to Serfdom". These intellectuals radically affected the thinking of Thatcher and Reagan, and brought about their developed economic policy. They successfully brought about the regeneration of the economy, and are just as relevant if not more relevant today than they were when they were influencing politicians in office.

If America seeks the change that Obama has been schooled in, and misguidedly advocates, it can lead only to ruin, at least in the long term. If it continues, a sixteen trillion dollar debt will only increase.

Here is Friedman speaking- and if Mr. Osborne or Mr. Cameron are reading this watch and learn- lest the end lead to the same disasters as the former Soviet Union.

https://www.youtube.com/watch?v=27Tf8RN3uiM&feature=plcp

Yours,

(for freedom and democracy)

Steven Parris Ward.

"Starbucks should avoid as much tax as it can": Alexandra Swann, Telegraph, Nov 24th 2012.

"When did taxation become a moral issue? Because it shouldn't be; it's just an irksome if almost unavoidable transaction between state and citizen, one that should be dramatically reduced."

Dear Miss Swann,

Your blog would have benefited from making a clear distinction between the franchisee and the franchisor. The franchisee pays taxes at the local level, whilst still paying a fee to the company to use the brand. The franchisor, being an international company, clearly feels it does not need to operate at the local level- it seeks the most favourable tax rates as a question of utility, in any given country of its choice, in order to continue functioning profitably.

There is a general question of a philosophical kind concerning whether acts of utility are good or bad/ moral or immoral; though that would take you beyond the scope of your blog. Briefly, it is addressed when you raise the issue of morality in reference to paying taxes. Early on, you appear to want to adopt the position that paying taxes is neither moral or immoral, as it is a mere "transaction". It is a position that some might adopt to argue there is no moral value or import to the market, as these are mere financial transactions, effected over and above moral choices made by individuals. Market forces are autonomous of individual desires or intentions. Alternatively, it could be argued, it is a fallacy to suppose that individuals can be divorced from the actions they perform, or the market can exist independently of the individuals that constitute it. In a similar fashion: universals must exist in some kind of relationship with particulars.

An erroneous version of these kind of arguments was raised against Thatcher when she claimed "there was no such thing as society". The view she adopted from Milton Friedman however, was not an emphasis that there were mere abstractions which should therefore be afforded no value, but that there were only individuals that comprised of these apparently abstract concepts that afforded them value. In Thatcher's case, her famous pronouncement would have been better served as: "There is no such thing as society over and above the individuals that give it value."

Your self-proclaimed "anarcho-libertarian" position at no time makes the case for paying no taxes, as anarchists and your critics on here have sometimes claimed. You simply imply the sensible view that less taxes should be paid to fund ever increasing State expenditure. This is a position eminently consistent with the libertarian position; with its emphasis on localism and less government control and power. Your implication that payment of taxes is an amoral act however, is one inconsistent with your view of libertarianism; with its emphasis on the importance of the individual, and his or her virtuous contribution to society.

Your later emphasis on "fairness" tends to undermine the amoral position, and suggests that there is a tax system that has a moral value. That rather flies in the face of your earlier amoral assertion.

Yours,

(for freedom and democracy)

Steven Parris Ward.

"I don't think it would be right for Britain"[to leave the EU]: reply to David Cameron, Telegraph Jan 6th, 2013.

"I don't think it would be right for Britain [to leave the EU]. My policy, my approach is determined absolutely, purely, and simply by the national interest. What is right for Britain? What is right for people in work? What's right for British business? What's right for the future of our country?" Prime Minister David Cameron 6th Jan 2013

So you believe that freedom, democracy, the right to decide our own laws and to practise our own jurisprudence is not in the national interest?

You prefer instead to be part of an organisation that shuns national democracies as being "populist". That labels democratic debate as "pointless semantics" [Barosso State of Union 2012] . You prefer to be a champion for Brussels to make 75% of our laws. To be a champion for further countries and immigrants to have the right to stay here.Countries such as Turkey which you campaign for and unstintingly support in future EU membership.

You prefer instead to be part of an organisation that favours taxation without democratic representation. An organisation that has threatened to impose fiscal taxes that threaten to destroy the British economy and the City of London. You prefer to be part of an organisation that some of its members consider should abolish her Majesty's government, who consider it an irrelevance and who have even labelled the inhabitants of this island and those who protest against such measures as being no more than dangerous nationalists and populists who should be repressed " [Barosso 2012] and by others to be no more than "Island monkeys" .

You prefer instead to dismantle our army, navy and airforce whilst you champion the European taskforce. You prefer to be limited in the ability to trade globally by EU legislation. You prefer as do most of the unelected "appointed" Commission rule from Brussels, and an end to intergovernmental decision making. You prefer instead the laws of the Lisbon Treaty that abolishes habeas corpus and favour rather the acquis communitaire legislation of the Treaty of Rome that made it legally binding for all member states to favour closer fiscal and political union, at least in principle.

You prefer to dine and make your bedfellows with former Soviet apparatchiks and criminals imprisoned for corruption. You prefer the company of former Soviets and Cultural Marxists and even Maoists such as Barosso who have never publically denounced their former radical ideologies.

You prefer these types even to the right wing members of your own "Conservative" party. How long before you label those Conservatives who were once your supporters fruitcakes, loonies and closet racists, simply because they espouse Conservative values? How can you call yourself a Conservative when you insult those essentially Thatcherite conservative UKIP supporters with such libellous, defamatory slurs?

You even claim one of your best friends is Obama, the son of Frank Marshall Davis a Communist Party extremist and poet, who still speaks of Saul Alinsky the radical agitator with admiration, along with Bill Ayres his Marxist comrade and imprisoned bomb terrorist.

You do all this in the interests of Britain's future you claim, whilst you deny the majority of the electorate their democratic right to a full in/out choice in a referendum. You have the gall to insult the British people's intelligence and condemn future generations to European Soviet style collectivist tyranny. You do this whilst you seek to dismantle this country its heritage and traditions against the people's will. And you have the gall to call this a democracy?

https://www.youtube.com/watch?v=YWSYMpuCFaQ

On the rights of gay marriage in Church: reply to Lord Tebbit, Jan 8th 2013.

"What is, to my mind at least certain is that if the qualification for marriage is widened to include persons of the same sex, the ECHR would be bound to rule that Churches or clergy refusing to perform marriage ceremonies were guilty of unlawful discrimination."

But that is exactly the point Lord Tebbit, it will be used in such a manner. Why is it being driven through, with no proper debate or white paper? Because it is being used by the globalists and the EU/ ECHR as a stick to drive us into a cul de sac of collectivist rule by an ever increasing, autocratic, undemocratic, corrupt mega state.

One thing these EU lairds in the Commission have in common is their use of an essentially Cultural Marxist strategy to undermine the Church, political institutions, education, etc. of national democracies. The attack on the nuclear family being another case in point, with single parent families being given financial rewards that encourage them to remain single parent families over the penalties imposed on married couples.

In respect of gay marriage by the Church, I myself am not a Christian. I also recognise the right of gays (a small minority) to enjoy the civil rights of law that other citizens do. But as British citizens, not *because* they are gay. I myself do not believe that sexual preference should be anything other than a private affair, and kept private if possible. It should not be a qualification for equal treatment, as much as it should not be a disqualification.

I do however also recognise that civil marriage is one thing and the religious ceremony that binds two people together through marriage in Church is another. In this respect, a Christian must, by virtue of their beliefs, accept two fundamental beliefs.

First that Jesus Christ was God incarnate died, rose again and in doing so expunged the world of its sin. Second, that the Bible is the eternal word of God.

With the latter premise in mind, the pronouncement in Leviticus that homosexuality is an "abomination to the eyes of the Lord", amongst other pronouncements such as St Paul's condemnation of it in the New Testament (the book of Romans), supports the view for Christians that it is a sinful act. It ensured also that the British Christian jurisprudence considered the practise was in fact a sin, and therefore illegal in this country until 1967.

The purpose of such promotions then by Cameron, and other political leaders on the continent and in the US, who paradoxically and hypocritically profess Christian beliefs is both a blasphemy and a down right lie. Further, it is an attack on the belief system of the Church and the Bible which they themselves profess to believe in and support. As an attack on the Church, it is one of many such attacks to undermine the institutions which further the Long March to a supposedly egalitarian utopia that in the past has been termed Communism. An ideal that history has shown to be a mere ideological carrot to a totalitarian state which does n't appear to collapse into a utopia; an ideology that has rather ensured the murder of millions, and the eventual containment of other protestors who oppose such group think in gulags.

With the current democratic deficit in the Commission at the moment, and their, in some cases, former Soviet sympathies and proven corruptions, I shall let readers draw their own conclusions as to where the EU is heading.

https://www.youtube.com/watch?v=YWSYMpuCFaQ

Yours

(for freedom and democracy)

Steven Parris Ward

http://blogs.telegraph.co.uk/news/normantebbit/100197031/yes-there-are-government-achievements-but-lib-dem-policies-are-still-being-forced-on-tories-by-their-own-prime-minister/

Alex Jones and the right to bear arms in the light of the Sandy Hook massacre: 8th January 2013.

Mr Jones is merely passionate not angry. Yes he is loud Piers, but since when was that wrong when you believe and love and seek to protect your country, as any good patriot should? His whole life has been led by such a raison d'etre.

He believes in the right of Americans to bear arms as per the second amendment and quite rightly so. Is Piers an American citizen? No. Whereas Jones is. He is in the middle of that passionate rant simply espousing the right of his fellow citizens to bear arms. Why? So that, as the Founding Fathers realised, being given such a right they might protect themselves from tyrannical governments that could seek to enslave and unlawfully tyrannise and threaten the people. By affording the people the right to bear arms America provides safety through empowerment for the individual from any aforesaid tyranny or emerging autocracy. Or in this case, for Jones, a New World Order, which appears to be increasingly emerging as an autocratic non democratic regime; at least in the EU. If you are Jones you also appear to be furnished with more than enough evidence to suggest such an emerging regime is developing plans to murder civilians.

The merits of the arguments for gun ownership, and the implications of whether this makes society safer or more dangerous can be debated with statistics. A terrible and tragic loss occurred. Children died. Yet, irrespective of gun laws, mentally ill murderer's will always find a way to secure the tools to bring about death. Ander's Breivik the Norweigian slayer is a testament to this in a country that does not espouse such gun ownership laws.

One thing is for sure, Piers Morgan has no right to seek to influence or change a country's present views, its constitution and laws, until he becomes a fully- fledged citizen. He is not, as a non-American citizen, afforded the same liberties or rights as an American in that country. He is no more than a guest. Criticising the said constitution as it presently is should be out of bounds to non-citizens who reside in the US until they become full US citizens. It is to the credit of the first amendment, part of a constitution he wishes to see dismantled, that he is afforded such a liberty and rights; to the credit of the tolerant views of the nation. In the meantime, he should be respectful, comply with the laws and not seek to incite constitutional change until such time as he is indeed an American citizen.

Considering all this and Morgan's reactions he should leave that country, and view his extended working holiday as a misfortunate one. As for my own personal preference, I hope he doesn't return to the UK. Or if he does he is forced to face the hacking scandal charges that caused him to flee in the first place.

http://blogs.telegraph.co.uk/news/edwest/100197174/alex-jones-a-synthesis-of-every-single-internet-commenter-on-earth/

Alex Jones is a nut because he believes Prozac is dangerous and governments are trying to kill us with it: reply to Tim Stanley, Telegraph 8th Jan 2013.

Concerning your first premise that Alex Jones is a "nut" based on the Prozac assertion.

Although antidepressants like Prozac are not technically considered to be addictive, at least in the sense of inducing cravings in patients, doctors say they do make users dependent. Drug dependency means that the body has adapted to a chemical to the point that it requires steady doses to normally function. Because of this, patients who abruptly stop taking antidepressant drugs are likely to experience withdrawal symptoms such as nausea, headache, dizziness and lethargy. Patients are warned to wean themselves off antidepressants slowly and under a doctor's care.

High doses of SSRIs often increase the severity of side effects, and one particular side effect can be fatal. The onset of Serotonin Syndrome, a condition in which too much of the mood elevator is present in the brain, can occur within minutes, producing high blood pressure, hyperthermia, high body temperature and an increased heart rate that can lead to shock. Serotonin Syndrome can arise when SSRIs act alone or in conjunction with other medication.

Prozac is one of the few antidepressants approved for the treatment of depression in youths. Unfortunately, however, studies on children have linked the drug to increased suicidal thoughts and behavior. As a result, the FDA issued a public warning in October 2004, and two years later extended the advisory to include young adults as old as 24.

In 2007, the FDA took an even stronger stance. The agency required antidepressant manufacturers to update existing black-box warnings about the increased risks of suicidal thoughts and behavior during initial treatment, which the FDA defined as the first one to two months.

An FDA black box warning is the most stringent precaution a drug can carry before it is pulled from the shelves. It takes its name from the black border that surrounds the warning information on the drug's packaging. The agency often requires pharmaceutical companies to include a bold warning on drug packaging and patient instruction sheets if serious or life-threatening risks are associated with the drug's use.

Clearly governments aren't trying to kill people with Prozac, but Prozac has health risks. Why then is it still being marketed and being permitted to be used by governments? Perhaps the profitability of the companies here outweighs the health risks?

A parallel can be drawn with the tobacco market which strong armed governments into denying the evidence of health risks for many decades before court causes sued the companies and the precedent for succesful suing was set in the 70's. Governments then quickly changed their tune and issued mandatory warnings.

Incidently, Dr. Stanley, smoking is a disgusting and dangerous habit for both smoker and anyone who passively inhales in the immediate vicinity. A famous victim, Roy Castle, died of cancer whilst yet being a non- smoker caused due to passive inhalation in Jazz clubs.

I suggest, therefore, you do us all a favour and give up (although it pains me to say it as a Libertarian).

http://www.timothystanley.co.uk/about-me.html

Yours

(for freedom and democracy)

Steven Parris Ward

(uncensored version)

Dear Dr. Stanley,

Please sir, distinguish between the dangers of Prozac and the theory or accusation that the governments are deliberately using it to kill people. There is still an issue here that

Jones quite rightly discusses. By labeling Jones a nut you sir, are simply dismissing out of hand the evidence provided by the FDA in 2004 and 2007 that led to Black Box warnings being issued on Prozac in recognition of its health risks. Empirical studies strongly suggest that Prozac increases the likelihood of suicide.

This of course does not mean governments are trying to kill people as Alex Jones suggests. The issue remains however: why is the government still permitting the marketing of Prozac by pharmaceutical companies when the health risks and dangers of increased suicide have been validated and supported by independent medical and FDA studies and validated with Black Box warnings? A case can therefore be made that the perpetuation of such a drug on the market by governments is tantamount to criminal neglect.

A parallel might be drawn with the tobacco companies and government responses or lack of them throughout the last century where they were muzzled into silence by the once highly profitable tobacco companies. It was not until tobacco companies were successfully sued in the 70's and the legal precedence was set that governments sought to provide government warnings on the dangers of tobacco smoking. Medical evidence and the link to cancer had been provided for decades previously and effectively ignored up until court cases successfully established a link.

US warns UK to stay in EU or risk "special relationship": 10th Jan 2013

This is the equivalent of the US urging a satellite of the USSR to remain within the Soviet Union during the Cold War when they desperately want democracy. All because they say it is in US interests. Whose interests exactly? These left wing US socialist schmucks actually sit there burbling on about liberty and freedom and the Arab Spring. Congratulating themselves at every opportunity that they are the land of the free and how wonderful their constitution is whilst they urge a country that gave them that constitution and the basic rules of law to remain within an undemocratic, corrupt cabal, where the people don't even get to vote for the President.

I'm too stunned and disappointed to comment further on our left wing American cousins.

Yours

(for freedom and democracy)

Steven Parris Ward

"And I do declare that no foreign prince, person, prelate, state or potentate hath or ought to have any jurisdiction, power, superiority, pre-eminence or authority, ecclesiastical or spiritual, within this realm."

English Bill of Rights, 1689.

www.ingramcontent.com/pod-product-compliance
Lightning Source LLC
Chambersburg PA
CBHW020348290526
45785CB00005B/2189